I0569961

THE K-POP PHENOMENON

ORIGINS, EVOLUTION, AND FUTURE — TRACE THE
HISTORY OF FIRST TO FIFTH-GENERATION IDOLS;
EXPLORE THE FORCES BEHIND THE GLOBAL
SENSATION

HALLYU PRESS

Cover design by Kostis Pavlou

To John Walter

The Jazz Age teacher who opened students' eyes to the fact that

history drives music while music drives history

CONTENTS

INTRO

How does a song you can't understand, performed by a singer you've never heard of — who's not even all that attractive by conventional standards, suddenly become the anthem of a global movement? That was what happened when PSY's "Gangnam Style" exploded onto the scene in 2012.

It didn't just become the first YouTube video to reach a billion views; it became the soundtrack to a cultural shift, introducing millions to the electrifying world of K-pop. But make no mistake. This wasn't a one-hit wonder. It was the tip of a much bigger iceberg, one that had been growing for decades beneath the surface.

Fast forward to 2024, and K-pop has transformed from a curious viral moment into one of the most influential forces in modern entertainment. Millions of fans worldwide stream Korean songs they may not understand, learn intricate dance moves from their favorite idols, and form powerful communities that span continents. But how did we get here? How did the music of a relatively obscure Asian nation in the shadows of its more prominent siblings become a cultural juggernaut that rivals – and often surpasses – Western pop music in global reach and influence?

K-pop isn't just a genre of music; it's a cultural phenomenon. Its influence stretches far beyond South Korea, touching lives and economies across the globe. From the bustling streets of Seoul to the concert arenas in Los Angeles, K-pop has a magnetic pull that's hard to resist. It influences fashion, language, and even international relations.

This book explores K-pop's history through chapters on its origins, evolution, key artists, and industry mechanics. We'll examine its global impact and cultural significance. We'll discover how K-pop became more than just music – it's a complete cultural ecosystem that encompasses fashion, beauty, technology, and social change.

A note to readers: you may notice some repetition as we revisit certain events or figures. This is intentional. K-pop's history, influenced by technological advances, socioeconomic factors, and globalization, is not made for a straightforward, linear narrative. Different "generations" of idols can only be understood within these overlapping contexts. We've structured the book to best capture this complex, interconnected story, occasionally weaving in fun facts to keep things engaging.

Who is this book for? It's for the passionate K-pop fans who live and breathe this genre. It's for the curious learners who want to understand what makes K-pop tick — or want to know why their teenage daughter suddenly became interested in learning the Korean language or started asking for Korean skincare products.

Whether you're a dedicated fan who knows every BTS choreography by heart, or simply curious about how a South Korean art form came to dominate global entertainment, this book offers an in-depth look at one of the most remarkable cultural phenomena of our time. Welcome to the world of K-pop – where tradition meets innovation, where East meets West, and where music continues to break down barriers we once thought impossible to cross.

CHAPTER 1

BEFORE K-POP
K-POP'S MUSICAL AND CULTURAL ROOTS

TURN on your favorite K-pop playlist and settle in. Behind those addictive beats and flawless performances that have millions of fans screaming worldwide, there's an incredible story waiting to be told. But it doesn't start with stadium concerts or viral music videos. K-pop's roots stretch back through centuries, blending ancient traditions with modern innovation, surviving historical challenges, and constantly reinventing itself to become the powerhouse genre we know today.

To truly appreciate the depth and complexity of K-pop, we must explore its roots. This journey takes us from the elegant courts of ancient Korea to the post-war streets of Seoul, from traditional melodies to Western-influenced rock, and from humble radio shows to spectacular televised performances. Each era, each genre, and each cultural shift has contributed to the unique sound and style that defines modern K-pop.

ECHOES OF THE PAST: TRADITIONAL KOREAN MUSIC

Long before stadium concerts and streaming platforms, music played an important role in Korean society. In the courtyards of ancient palaces, singers performed *gagok*, a beautiful and complex style of vocal music that showed just how sophisticated Korean art could be. These weren't simple performances – solo singers, backed by traditional instruments like the *geomungo* (a six-stringed zither) and *daegeum* (bamboo flute), had to master incredibly difficult pieces that required both technical skill and deep emotional expression. This wasn't just about entertainment – these performances were the height of cultural achievement, bringing together poetry, music, and scholarly traditions in one stunning art form.

The complexity of *gagok* performances required years of dedicated study. Vocalists mastered intricate ornamentations called *sigimsae*, which involved subtle pitch modifications and rhythmic variations. These techniques find modern parallels in the melismatic singing styles —singing multiple notes on a single syllable — of K-pop ballads, where artists like EXO's Chen and MAMAMOO's Solar demonstrate similar vocal agility and control.

Beyond palace walls, **pansori** captured the hearts of common people. This unique storytelling art form featured a lone singer (*sorikkun*) accompanied by a drummer (*gosu*), weaving epic tales through powerful vocals and dramatic gestures. The demanding vocal techniques of *pansori*, requiring years of rigorous training to achieve its characteristic husky timbre, find modern echoes in the intensive vocal training of K-pop idols. Today's elaborate K-pop music videos and concept albums mirror *pansori's* tradition of narrative storytelling through music.

Pansori performers often trained in isolated mountain areas, practicing until their voices became raw and developed the distinctive "bitter" quality (*sureong*) prized in the art form. This dedication to perfecting one's craft parallels the grueling training periods modern K-pop trainees undergo, sometimes lasting five to seven years before debut.

Fun Fact: BTS is said to have incorporated traditional Korean instruments and vocal techniques influenced by pansori *in the intro and bridge in "Idol."*

The Rich Assortment of Traditional Instruments

Traditional Korean instruments helped shape what would eventually become K-pop's rich, layered sound. The versatile *gayageum* (12-stringed zither) could express emotions from profound sorrow to explosive joy, while percussion ensembles called *samulnori* created complex rhythmic patterns that resonate in today's dynamic K-pop beats. The four key instruments of *samulnori* – *kkwaenggwari* (small gong), *janggu* (hourglass drum), *buk* (barrel drum), and *jing* (large gong) – established rhythmic traditions that continue to influence contemporary Korean music production.

Traditional Korean music emphasized the concept of *heung* – a state of collective joy and excitement generated through music and dance. This spiritual and emotional elevation through performance directly influences modern K-pop's emphasis on creating euphoric concert experiences and fostering strong emotional connections with audiences.

A TIME OF CHANGE: MUSIC UNDER JAPANESE OCCUPATION (1910-1945)

The year 1910 marked the beginning of **Japanese colonial rule in Korea**, a period that would last for 35 years and leave an indelible mark on every aspect of Korean society, including its music.

Under Japanese rule, traditional Korean music faced severe restrictions. The colonial government imposed strict measures to suppress Korean culture and promote Japanese customs. Many traditional Korean instruments and songs were banned or heavily restricted, forcing musicians to either adapt to Japanese styles or go underground to preserve their heritage.

But Korean music didn't simply disappear or hide; it evolved. One of the most significant introductions during this period was *enka*, a genre of Japanese popular music. *Enka's* melancholic melodies and heartfelt lyrics resonated with many Koreans, who found themselves in a state of cultural and emotional turmoil. Korean musicians began to incorporate elements of *enka* into their work, blending Japanese musical styles with their own.

Yet, music also became a powerful form of resistance. Underground, a vibrant scene of protest songs emerged. These patriotic tunes, often performed in secret, kept Korean identity alive during the darkest times. Music became more than entertainment; it was a lifeline of cultural continuity and a beacon of hope.

The legacy of this period in Korean music is complex. It represents both a time of cultural suppression and a catalyst for musical innovation. This duality - the pain of oppression and the creativity born from adversity - continues to echo in the intricate harmonies and powerful performances of modern K-pop.

FROM WAR TO REVIVAL: THE BIRTH OF KOREAN POP (1950S-1960S)

The end of Japanese rule in 1945 didn't bring immediate peace to the Korean peninsula. Barely five years after emerging from colonial rule, the nation was thrust into another catastrophic conflict. **The Korean War** (1950-1953) erupted when North Korean forces, supported by the Soviet

Union and China, invaded South Korea on June 25, 1950. The United States and United Nations forces quickly came to South Korea's aid, leading to a devastating three-year struggle that claimed millions of lives and left the Korean peninsula divided at the 38th parallel—a division that persists to this day.

In the wake of this brutal conflict, South Korea faced the monumental task of rebuilding a shattered nation. It was in this context of national trauma and the struggle for recovery that music emerged as a powerful force for healing and unity.

A musical genre called *Trot* (트로트) became the soundtrack of South Korea's post-war era. *Trot* represented a unique fusion of musical influences, blending elements of traditional Korean melodies with Japanese *Enka* and newfound American influences brought by the presence of the U.S. military.

Two artists became iconic voices of the post-war *Trot* era: Lee Mi-ja and Nam Jin. Lee Mi-ja's 1964 hit "Camellia Lady" (동백 아가씨), despite being banned at the time for its melancholic tone, resonated deeply with many Koreans. The song's metaphor comparing the resilient camellia flower to the enduring spirit of the Korean people struck a chord with listeners. Nam Jin, known for his soulful voice and charismatic stage presence, added new emotional layers to *Trot*.

Meanwhile, the presence of American military bases in South Korea became a significant conduit for Western musical influences. The **American Forces Korea Network (AFKN)** introduced Koreans to a wide array of Western music, from jazz and rock to pop.

The 1960s saw the rise of rock music in South Korea. Bands like **The Add4** and **Key Boys** emerged, bringing the energy of rock 'n' roll to Korean audiences. **Shin Joong-hyun**, often called the "Godfather of Korean Rock," played a pivotal role in this movement. His band, The Add4, was among the first to introduce the electric guitar to Korean audiences, revolutionizing the local music scene.

During this era, the **Kim Sisters** became one of the first Korean acts to achieve success in the United States. Initially performing at American military bases in Korea, they eventually gained popularity stateside, making numerous appearances on iconic TV programs like *The Ed Sullivan Show*. Their success showcased Korean talent to international audiences and, in turn, exposed South Korea to

Western music styles, contributing to the evolving local music scene.

THE WESTERN WAVE: ROCK, BALLADS, AND THE BEGINNINGS OF K-POP (1970S-EARLY 1990S)

As Korea continued to modernize in the 1970s and 1980s, the music scene saw a significant shift. Western pop music firmly established its presence, with artists like Michael Jackson and Madonna becoming household names in South Korea.

This period laid the groundwork for the emergence of modern K-pop. Artists like **Cho Yong-pil** played a key role in this transition, blending Western pop and rock elements with Korean musical styles. His polished production and broad appeal helped popularize contemporary Korean music, paving the way for the idol-driven K-pop wave that would follow a decade later.

The 1980s ushered in a new era of Korean ballads that challenged Trot's dominance. Drawing inspiration from Western music while maintaining distinctly Korean sensibilities, artists like Cho Yong-pil and **Lee Moon-sae** pioneered this emerging style. Their songs—such as Cho's "The Woman Outside the Window" and Lee's "Old Love"—became cultural touchstones, their poignant melodies and introspective lyrics reflecting the complexities of modern Korean society.

The fusion of Western and Korean musical elements created a rich blend of sounds. Korean musicians adopted Western instruments like the electric guitar, drum set, and synthesizer, incorporating them into their compositions. This wasn't mere imitation; it was a creative blending that retained the essence of Korean musical traditions.

Fun Fact: South Korea's rapid economic rise from the 1960s to the 1990s was dubbed the Miracle on the Han River. *In a few decades, South Korea transformed itself from post-war poverty to a global economic powerhouse, with Seoul's Han River region symbolizing this impressive growth.*

THE POWER OF THE AIRWAVES: BROADCASTING AND THE SHAPING OF K-POP

As Korean popular music evolved, broadcasting networks played a pivotal role in shaping the country's music scene. The **Korean Broadcasting System (KBS)**, established in 1927, initially led this revolution as the first national radio broadcaster, bringing music into homes across the nation. Through radio, KBS made a diverse range of musical genres accessible to the public, helping to democratize music consumption at a time when not everyone had access to live performances.

In 1961, the **Munhwa Broadcasting Corporation (MBC)** emerged, quickly becoming known for its focus on entertainment. MBC's radio programs, alongside KBS's, became launchpads for new artists, influencing public tastes and helping to introduce emerging genres and artists to listeners across South Korea.

Radio shows served as the primary medium for the spread of music throughout the 1950s and 1960s. However, as technology advanced, **television** began to overshadow radio. This transition brought about a major shift in how music was experienced, turning it into a visual as well as an auditory medium.

By the late 70s, shows like *MBC Singing Stations* brought live performances into homes across the country, letting audiences watch their favorite artists perform rather than just hear them on the radio. For the first time, viewers could see everything – the expressions, the stage presence, the fashion – creating a deeper connection between fans and artists.

Then came *Gayo Top 10*. Think of it as the 1980s Korean version of *Billboard Hot 100* or TikTok's viral charts today. Launched by KBS in 1981, this weekly TV show counted down the hottest songs in Korea, much like music shows *M Countdown* or *Music Bank* do now. Artists would perform their latest hits, competing for the top spot, and the whole country would tune in to see who made it to #1. Getting a high ranking on *Gayo Top 10* could make or break a song's success – boosting album sales and turning unknown artists into overnight sensations. It wasn't just a TV show; it was where Korean music trends were born.

The evolution continued into the 1990s, with the advent of specialized music shows like *Inkigayo* (1991) and *Music Bank* (1998). These programs further solidified the importance of televised music performances. Weekly live stages and competitive rankings made television an essential part of an artist's career, serving as barometers of success in the industry. These shows were instrumental in promoting the emerging K-pop idol culture, where visuals, dance, and stagecraft became just as important as vocal performance.

Other iconic shows enriched this landscape even further. For example, the *KBS National Singing Contest*, which started in 1980, brought a unique approach by traveling to various regions of South Korea, giving local talents a chance to shine on a national stage. This program helped many artists gain their first taste of national exposure and remains a beloved institution.

As the new millennium approached, the lines between music and other forms of entertainment began to blur. **Variety shows** like *Happy Together* (2001) and *Running Man* (2010) regularly featured idol groups and solo artists, allowing fans to see a different side of their favorites. Idol groups had to prove themselves as entertainers, capable of adapting to the challenges and fast-paced nature of these shows.

Broadcasting's influence on Korean music went beyond just music shows. Commercial jingles became hit songs, and K-drama soundtracks topped the charts when fans fell in love with the music from their favorite shows. This close relationship between TV and music created something special in Korea – where a song wasn't just a song, but part of a larger entertainment experience.

This powerful combination of TV and music worked perfectly for everyone involved. TV networks got fresh performances and content for their shows, while artists gained new ways to reach fans. This symbiotic system helped develop new talent, encouraged creative ideas, and set the stage for K-pop to become the global phenomenon it is today.

THE CULTURAL CONTEXT: THE VALUES THAT SHAPED K-POP

Understanding K-pop requires looking deeper into Korean culture and values. These cultural foundations have profoundly shaped both how the K-pop industry operates and how its artists view their roles as performers and public figures.

Confucianism: A Legacy of Hierarchy and Respect

For centuries, Korean society has been shaped by Confucianism, a set of beliefs and values that originated in China. These principles became so woven into Korean culture that they still influence how people interact today. At its core, Confucianism values **respect for authority, dedication to family**, and putting **group harmony ahead of individual desires**.

These values are especially visible in K-pop's seniority system, where younger artists (*hubae*) show clear respect to their seniors (*sunbae*). Whether it's bowing to senior artists backstage or letting them speak first in interviews, these traditions help maintain harmony and unity within groups and industry as a whole. This structure of respect doesn't just apply to interactions between different groups – even within the same group, younger members follow the lead of older ones, creating the discipline and teamwork that K-pop is famous for.

Confucian values also emphasize the importance of constantly working to improve yourself. This explains a lot about K-pop's intense training system – where spending years perfecting your singing, dancing, and language skills isn't just expected, it's celebrated. When you hear about K-pop trainees practicing for 12+ hours a day or see BTS still taking dance lessons at the height of their success, you're witnessing this ancient cultural value in action. It's not just about working hard; it's about the deep-rooted belief that there's always room to get better.

A Culture of Hard Work and High Expectations

South Korea is famous for its "work hard" culture – it's not just about doing your best; it's about being the best. This mindset helped transform the country from one of the world's poorest in the 1950s into the economic powerhouse we see today. In Korean, they call this dedicated work ethic *geunmu* (근무), and you can see it everywhere, from schools to workplaces to K-pop training rooms.

Take education, for example. Korean students don't just go to regular school – many spend their evenings at *hagwons* (after-school academies) studying until late at night. They're competing to get into the best high schools and universities, just like K-pop trainees compete for debut spots in their companies. Imagine spending your whole day at school, then studying until midnight, then doing it all again tomorrow. That's normal life for many Korean teens.

This intense drive for success has a special name in Korean: *yeolsimhi* (열심히) – which means giving 100% to everything you do. For K-pop idols, this means:

- Practicing dance routines until they're perfect
- Training their voices for hours every day
- Learning multiple languages to connect with international fans
- Maintaining a flawless public image

- Always staying competitive in a crowded industry

Sounds exhausting? It is. Just like students struggling with exam stress, idols often face burnout from these intense expectations. While this work ethic has created some of K-pop's biggest successes, it also shows how challenging the path to stardom really is.

AT ITS CORE, K-pop embodies centuries of Korean culture. Its famously rigorous training reflects traditional Confucian values, while its spectacular performances build on Korea's long artistic heritage. K-pop's talent for innovation mirrors a culture that has always adapted to change while keeping its identity intact. So while K-pop videos and concerts might seem entirely modern, they're actually fresh expressions of deeply Korean values and traditions - proof that global appeal can grow from authentic local roots.

CHAPTER 2

THE BIRTH OF K-POP

THE PIONEERS AND THE FIRST-GENERATION K-POP STARS: 1990S-EARLY 2000S

AS THE 1990S began in Seoul, one could sense that something big was about to happen. The city was changing fast - new buildings rising everywhere, young people buzzing with energy and fresh ideas. South Korea was on the cusp of a cultural transformation, and within this dynamic atmosphere, a musical phenomenon was about to emerge. This is the story of K-pop's birth, a tale of creativity, resilience, and a nation's drive to reinvent itself.

THE DAWN OF A NEW ERA: SOUTH KOREA IN THE 1990S

Here is a picture of Seoul, a bustling metropolis where old meets new, in the early 90's. The streets are buzzing with construction noise and energy - the sound of a country transforming itself. South Korea had finally become a true democracy, and you could feel the excitement everywhere.

The year 1992 marked a pivotal moment in South Korean history. After more than three decades of military rule, South Korea elected a civilian president, Kim Young-sam, who took office in 1993. At his inauguration, he said something South Koreans had waited generations to hear: "Today, we are entering **a new era of civilian democracy** in which the people are the true masters of the country."

A wave of optimism and open-mindedness swept across South Korea. Young people packed into cafes and parks, freely talking about things that would've been risky to discuss just a few years before - politics, art, their dreams for the future. The whole country felt like it was finally breathing freely, ready to create something new.

This change in politics changed everything. Artists who'd been censored for years could finally express themselves freely. Musicians started experimenting with new styles, whether they were working in basement studios or fancy corporate buildings. Korean music was about to explode with creativity.

When Korea Got Rich, Pop Culture Exploded

As South Korea's economy boomed and Seoul filled with skyscrapers, young people wanted entertainment made in Korea, for Korea. The city was ultra-modern, with fast internet and massive shopping districts. The rise of consumer culture meant that Korean youth weren't just looking for basic stuff anymore - they wanted experiences that would let them express themselves and have fun.

This new generation had something their parents didn't really have: **time and money to spend on entertainment**. They were educated, tech-savvy, and hungry for fresh, innovative music. Entertainment companies noticed this untapped market and started experimenting with new styles of pop music that would appeal to these young, urban listeners.

Korea's Internet Revolution: Setting the Stage

In the mid-1990s, while most countries were just getting dial-up internet, South Korea went all-in on high-speed connections. By the end of the decade, walk into any Seoul internet café (called "*PC bang*"), and it felt like stepping into the future. Young people could hop online, share music, and connect with others who loved the same artists.

This super-fast internet turned out to be perfect for K-pop. While other countries were still figuring out digital music, Korean entertainment companies were already sharing high-quality music videos and connecting with fans online. With this **"digital-first" approach**, i.e., making everything available online from the start, K-pop was ready to go global in a way that other music scenes weren't, allowing fans world-wide to access performances, music videos, and behind-the-scenes content with incredible ease.

Creating a New Kind of Music

At night, Seoul came alive with music pouring out of every club, café, and corner. Young Korean musicians were taking what they loved about

American hip-hop, R&B, and pop, but putting their own spin on it. They weren't just copying Western music - they were creating something new that felt uniquely Korean.

All over the city, artists were trying out this fresh style. They mixed elements from different types of music, not afraid to experiment and break rules. This creative freedom and willingness to try new things would eventually lead to what we now know as K-pop - a style that would go on to take over the world.

SEO TAIJI AND BOYS: THE REVOLUTIONARIES

In the midst of all this, something seismic happened on MBC's popular TV talent show on April 11, 1992. Three young men, dressed in baggy clothes and backward caps, stood before the cameras. The music started, and within seconds, it became apparent that something extraordinary was happening.

This was Seo Taiji and Boys, and they were about to change Korean music forever.

The Performance That Shook the Nation

As Seo Taiji, Yang Hyun-suk, and Lee Juno launched into their debut song, "Nan Arayo (I Know)," the studio audience was initially stunned into silence. The song was unlike anything they'd heard before – a dynamic blend of rap, hip-hop, and dance rhythms, breaking away from the conventional styles of Korean pop music at the time.

Seo Taiji's powerful vocals cut through the air, his lyrics touching on social issues that resonated deeply with the youth in the audience. The choreography was sharp and energetic, with moves borrowed from American hip-hop but infused with a uniquely Korean flair.

As the performance ended, there was a moment of silence... and then the studio erupted. The applause was deafening, the cheers almost desperate in their intensity. In living rooms across Korea, viewers sat stunned, many rewinding their VCRs to watch the performance again and again.

Fun Fact: The judges on that fateful evening clearly did not understand what hit them. They gave Seo Taiji and Boys the lowest score of the night! Obviously, everybody else disagreed.

The Aftermath: A Cultural Earthquake

In the days and weeks that followed, "Nan Arayo" became a national sensation. It topped charts, dominated radio play, and sparked fierce debates in schools and offices across the country. Some older Koreans were shocked by the group's unconventional style and message, but for the country's youth, it finally felt like someone got them.

As Seo Taiji and Boys released more music, their influence only grew. Each new song pushed the boundaries further, introducing Korean audiences to genres like rap-rock, techno, and hardcore.

Their 1994 song "Classroom Idea" became an anthem for students frustrated with Korea's rigid education system. The lyrics, sharp and unapologetic, resonated with millions:

"Why is there nothing but studying? It's as if I'm a parrot learning to speak. What's the difference between man and machine? If there's nothing but the need to raise our grades…"

The controversial lyrics led to **bans** on public broadcasts and **censorship**, but the song sparked a national conversation about education reform, demonstrating the power of music to drive social change.

It wasn't just about the music, though. Everywhere you looked, Korean teens were copying their hip-hop style and streetwear. More importantly, young people were following their lead in speaking up about society's problems.

Seo Taiji and Boys didn't just change what people listened to or how they dressed. Their willingness to address social issues in their lyrics inspired a generation to think critically about the world around them.

The Legacy: Laying the Foundation for K-pop

As they say, all good things must come to an end. In 1996, at the height of their popularity, Seo Taiji and Boys announced that they were breaking up. Fans were devastated, but they had already changed Korean music forever, and had laid the foundation for a new era of South Korean pop culture.

Seo Taiji and Boys were like the grandparents of today's K-pop. The way they mixed different music styles, their bold fashion choices, and how they weren't afraid to speak up about social issues - all of this became the DNA of modern K-pop. The artists you know today, from BTS to BLACKPINK, are building on what Seo Taiji and Boys started. They showed that Korean pop music could be more than just entertainment - it could say something important while still being incredibly popular.

THE RISE OF IDOL GROUPS: H.O.T. AND SECHS KIES

As the dust settled from the Seo Taiji and Boys phenomenon, everyone was hungry for the next big thing in Korean music. The appetite for fresh, youth-driven music was insatiable, but how could the music industry take advantage of this newfound momentum? Lee Soo-man, a former folk singer and visionary, believed he had the answer.

Through his company SM Entertainment, Lee envisioned a new, systematized approach to creating pop stars from the ground up. He wasn't just looking for talented singers - he wanted to create complete entertainers who could sing, dance, and capture people's hearts. His plan? Take young performers, train them intensively in everything from dancing to languages, and turn them into polished superstars. This was the beginning of what we now know as K-pop idol groups.

The Birth of the K-pop Idol: H.O.T.

In 1996, SM Entertainment launched H.O.T. (High-five Of Teenagers), introducing the first modern "**idol group**" in the K-pop sense. This group wasn't just a band; it was a carefully crafted phenomenon aimed at young audiences. The five members were handpicked and rigorously trained to be perfect pop stars. Inspired by the Japanese concept of "idols," which referred to popular entertainers, H.O.T. gave this idea a distinctly Korean twist. Each member had a unique role and personality, allowing fans to choose their own favorites, a formula that would soon become a hallmark of K-pop.

Their debut single, "Candy," became an instant hit with its catchy melody and playful lyrics. But it wasn't just the song that drew fans in—H.O.T.'s synchronized dance routines, flashy outfits, and carefully crafted images made for a complete package that appealed to young people throughout Korea.

Intense Fan Culture Emerges

As H.O.T.'s popularity skyrocketed, a new phenomenon emerged: the super fan. These dedicated followers, mostly teenage girls, organized themselves with military-like discipline and precision. Known as "Club H.O.T.," they turned H.O.T. concerts into spectacles of synchronized chanting, unwavering enthusiasm, and coordinated white outfits, creating vast seas of white—the official color of H.O.T.—which became a signature feature of the group's performances.

This intense fan culture wasn't limited to concerts. Fans were meticulous in tracking every detail of the idols' lives—from their fashion choices to their public appearances. This level of devotion and organization laid the groundwork for what would become a defining feature of K-pop: the passionate, organized, and loyal fandom.

Fun Fact: H.O.T fans also waved white balloons to the beat of the music — basically inventing what would later become those glowing light-sticks you see at every K-pop concert today.

Enter Sechs Kies: The Birth of K-pop Rivalries

Success invites competition. After H.O.T. became such a big hit, other companies raced to develop their own idol groups. Among them was DSP Media, which launched Sechs Kies ("six crystals" in German) in 1997.

From the start, Sechs Kies was marketed as direct rivals to H.O.T. While H.O.T. represented polished appeal, Sechs Kies adopted a tougher, more rebellious image, positioning themselves as the "bad boys" of K-pop. Their debut single, "School Anthem," featured a bold sound and lyrics that spoke up against Korea's rigid education system, resonating with students who felt overwhelmed by the pressure of academic expectations.

Sechs Kies quickly amassed a dedicated fanbase. Known as the "Yellow Kies" due to their use of yellow balloons and outfits at concerts, these fans became the passionate counterparts to H.O.T.'s loyal "Club H.O.T."

The Great Idol War

The rivalry between H.O.T. and Sechs Kies in the 1990s wasn't just about music - it became a massive cultural movement that divided young people in Korea into two passionate camps. It was a defining moment in K-pop history, where choosing your favorite group became part of your identity.

The competition between fans went beyond the social media arguments we see today. There were actual physical confrontations between H.O.T.'s fanbase (Club H.O.T.) and Sechs Kies' supporters (Yellow Kies) at schools and concerts. The media amplified this rivalry, turning each album release into a major event. Fans would buy multiple copies of albums to help their group achieve higher sales rankings - a practice that is still seen in K-pop culture today.

This intense competition had an unexpected positive effect: it pushed both groups to constantly improve. They developed more complex choreography, produced better music, and created more impressive performances. Without realizing it, H.O.T. and Sechs Kies were setting new standards for what would become the global K-pop industry. The high-production performances and intense fan culture that define modern K-pop can be traced back to this rivalry.

THE FIRST GENERATION EXPANDS: DIVERSE VOICES IN K-POP

By the late 1990s, K-pop was blowing up thanks to groups like H.O.T. and Sechs Kies. Their success opened the doors for a wide range of artists. While boy groups dominated the scene initially, female idols soon made their mark.

Breaking New Ground: Enter the Girl Groups

In late 1997, three talented young women called **S.E.S.** (Sea, Eugene, and Shoo) stepped into the spotlight. They were created by SM Entertainment - the same company behind H.O.T. Their first song, "I'm Your Girl," showed everyone that girl groups could be just as impactful as the boys.

S.E.S. brought something totally different to K-pop. While the boy groups were doing intense hip-hop tracks, S.E.S. focused on smooth R&B and pop melodies. They had a polished, sweet image, but their dancing and singing skills were impressive.

Then, in 1998, DSP Media launched **Fin.K.L**, featuring four members. These women came with a more grown-up, sophisticated vibe. Their songs hit different - they had powerful vocals and emotional depth that really connected with fans.

Just like H.O.T. and Sechs Kies had their rivalry, S.E.S. and Fin.K.L became competing forces in K-pop. Both groups kept pushing each other to do better, setting higher standards for female performers. Along the way, they proved something important: girl groups could be just as successful and influential as boy groups. Without S.E.S. and Fin.K.L, we might not have groups like BLACKPINK and TWICE today.

At the same time, **Baby V.O.X.**, another girl group under DR Music, was carving its niche with a bolder, edgier style. Known for their sleek visuals, Baby V.O.X. pushed boundaries for female idols, emphasizing a mix of sex appeal and vocal talent. They also gained attention internationally, particularly in China, marking an early step toward K-pop's global influence.

Solo Stars Shine: The Rise of BoA and Rain

While groups dominated K-pop's early years, two solo artists came along and made their mark.

Enter **BoA** in 2000 - imagine being just 13 years old and already showing the talent of a seasoned pro. SM Entertainment (the same company behind H.O.T. and S.E.S.) saw something special in her, and they were right. BoA could sing, dance, and command attention like few others, quickly earning her nickname "Queen of K-pop."

But what made BoA truly revolutionary was her international success. Instead of just focusing on Korea, she recorded songs in Korean, Japanese, and English. This was groundbreaking - especially in Japan, where foreign artists rarely succeeded. In 2002, she did something no Korean artist had ever done before: her album *Listen to My Heart* hit #1 on the *Oricon* music chart ("Japan's *Billboard*").

Then in 2002, along came Rain (Jung Ji-hoon). If BoA was the queen, Rain became K-pop's new king. Under JYP Entertainment, he brought something fresh: incredible dancing, smooth vocals, and the kind of stage presence that made it impossible to look away. He didn't just stay in Korea - his crossover success in markets like China and Japan hinted at K-pop's growing potential for global reach. He even made some strides in the United States, performing at the Madison Square Garden Theater and landing roles in Hollywood films like *Speed Racer* and *Ninja Assassin*.

Together, BoA and Rain showed that K-pop artists could succeed solo and, more importantly, that Korean entertainment could work worldwide. They helped pave the way for today's global K-pop stars.

Meanwhile, **PSY** made his debut during this era in 2001 with a quirky, satirical approach to music that stood out from the polished idols of the time. While his global breakout with "Gangnam Style" wouldn't come until years later, PSY's unique style and sharp humor laid the groundwork for his later success, showing the diversity in what K-pop could be.

K-pop Branches Out: More Than Just Dance Pop

By the late '90s, K-pop was growing beyond just pop groups with synchronized dancing. Different musical styles started making their mark, giving fans more variety to choose from.

Take **Nell**, who debuted in 1999. While most K-pop was upbeat and flashy, Nell came in with a totally different vibe—think alternative rock with deep lyrics and moody melodies. They were more like Coldplay than typical K-pop groups, offering something for fans who wanted music with a different kind of emotional depth.

Then there was **1TYM** (pronounced "One Time"), who brought real hip-hop into K-pop in 1998. Under YG Entertainment (the same company that would later give us BIGBANG and BLACKPINK), members Teddy Park, Oh Jinhwan, Song Baekkyoung, and Danny Im were doing something closer to American hip-hop. Their style helped pave the way for the rap-heavy K-pop we hear today in groups like Stray Kids and BTS.

In 1998, **Shinhwa** debuted, quickly setting themselves apart with their versatility. While starting with a dance-pop formula, they soon incorporated R&B, hip-hop, and ballads into their music. Tracks like "T.O.P." and "Perfect Man" showcased smooth vocals and powerful choreography, while later albums embraced more mature, musically rich concepts. Their adaptability and longevity proved that K-pop idols could grow with their audience, inspiring future generations.

In 1999, **g.o.d. (Groove Over Dose)** showed up with strong R&B influences. Instead of focusing on dance hits, they became famous for emotional ballads that told real stories about family and everyday life struggles. They were the R&B storytellers of K-pop—their songs connected with people of all ages because they sang about experiences everyone could relate to.

In the same year, **Fly to the Sky** debuted as SM Entertainment's first duo, making a bold statement in a sea of boy and girl groups. Their music leaned heavily on R&B ballads, focusing on heartfelt lyrics and vocal harmonies rather than flashy choreography. Songs like "Sea of Love" and "Missing You" stood out for their emotional depth and polished production, appealing to fans who craved a more introspective side of K-pop. Their success helped popularize R&B as a core element of the industry's musical repertoire.

These groups proved that K-pop could be more than just one thing—it could include rock, hip-hop, R&B, and pretty much any style of music, as long as it connected with people. Many of today's K-pop groups mix all these styles together, but these artists were among the first to break the mold.

THE FIRST GENERATION: A FOUNDATION FOR THE FUTURE

The year 2000 marked a turning point when K-pop evolved from simple music into a powerful cultural movement.

Seoul's streets reflected K-pop's growing influence. Giant billboards of idol groups dominated street corners. Their music streamed from shop speakers, becoming the city's everyday soundtrack, much like how pop hits fill Times Square today.

The internet transformed fan culture. Dedicated followers packed into internet cafes (*PC bangs*) to connect online, sharing photos and news about their favorite artists. These early online communities formed the blueprint for today's digital K-pop fandom.

Between classes, students practiced idol dance moves in schoolyards. K-pop had become more than music - young people emulated everything about their favorite stars, from choreography to fashion.

The first K-pop stars wielded significant cultural influence. When H.O.T.'s Tony Ahn dyed his hair blonde, it sparked a nationwide trend. Fin.K.L's **Lee Hyori**'s bold fashion choices inspired young women to express themselves more confidently.

These artists addressed serious topics too. Groups like g.o.d and Seo Taiji and Boys wrote lyrics about real issues - academic pressure, social norms, and politics. They sparked important conversations among youth about society and culture.

As these first-generation stars matured, many expanded into television and acting. This evolution helped K-pop grow beyond music into a comprehensive entertainment industry. These pioneers created the foundation for today's global K-pop scene, where artists like BTS and BLACKPINK influence culture worldwide, just as their predecessors did in Korea.

CHAPTER 3

THE KOREAN WAVE AND K-POP
THE RISE OF HALLYU

BEFORE WE CONTINUE TRACING K-pop's generational journey, let's pause to explore the cultural wave that has propelled it to global shores. In the early 2000s, South Korea pulled off something pretty incredible - they turned their culture into one of their biggest exports. This movement got a special name: "Hallyu" (한류) or "The Korean Wave."

But Hallyu wasn't just about K-pop hitting the charts worldwide. It was bigger than that - Korean TV shows (K-dramas), movies, food, fashion, and beauty products started catching on globally. Suddenly, people everywhere were learning Korean, trying Korean skincare routines, and craving Korean BBQ.

The timing was perfect. As the internet made the world more connected, Korea was ready with amazing content. While the first generation of K-pop stars (like H.O.T. and S.E.S.) had mainly focused on Asia, the following generations would ride this Korean Wave to worldwide fame.

This cultural explosion didn't just happen by accident - **Korea made it happen on purpose.** After facing tough economic times in the late 1990s, the country realized that entertainment and culture could be as valuable as manufacturing phones or cars. They invested heavily in their entertainment industry, and that bet paid off big time.

Understanding Hallyu helps explain why groups like BTS and BLACK-PINK became global sensations. They weren't just random success stories

- they were part of a bigger movement that turned Korean pop culture into a worldwide phenomenon.

Fun Fact: The term "Hallyu" was popularized by Chinese journalists in the late 1990s when they noticed Korean dramas and music rapidly gaining popularity in China.

FROM ECONOMIC CRISIS TO CULTURAL POWER MOVE

In 1997, South Korea faced a serious economic challenge. **The Asian Financial Crisis** struck a blow to the entire region, and suddenly, this country - known for manufacturing giants like Samsung and Hyundai - found itself in severe financial trouble. Their once-strong economy took a dramatic downturn.

But instead of just focusing on rebuilding their traditional industries, Korea's leaders made a bold decision. They looked at their entertainment industry - the music, TV shows, and movies - and recognized its untapped potential as a valuable export.

The strategy was groundbreaking: While other countries focused on traditional exports during the economic recovery, Korea chose to invest heavily in its creative industries. They realized that entertainment could be as valuable an export as smartphones or cars.

This decision to invest in entertainment and culture was pretty revolutionary at the time. Most countries dealing with economic problems wouldn't think, "Let's pour money into making pop stars." But Korea saw the potential in their creative industries, and this think-outside-the-box approach laid the groundwork for what would become a global cultural phenomenon.

When Korea Turned Pop Culture into a Science

As the government led by President Kim Dae-jung decided to make Korean culture famous worldwide, at the same time, **Lee Soo-man** (the mastermind behind SM Entertainment) came up with a wild concept - he called it **"Cultural Technology."**

Just as Samsung had a specific process for making high-tech phones, Lee figured they could create a systematic way to make hit songs and global stars. It wasn't just about making music - it was about creating a whole formula for success.

The idea was innovative yet straightforward: Treat cultural content like a technology that could be developed, refined, and marketed globally. Just as Samsung and LG dominated electronics, Korea aimed to become a leader in cultural exports.

The government loved this idea and lent its support with four major moves:

1. **Financial Incentives**: They gave entertainment companies tax breaks and subsidies - enabling companies like SM Entertainment and YG Entertainment to take bigger risks in promoting their artists internationally, e.g., sending their artists overseas to perform.
2. **Better Venues**: Recognizing the need for world-class facilities, the government invested in venues like the Seoul Olympic Stadium, which became a vital hub for large-scale K-pop concerts, helping the industry put on the kind of spectacular shows they're now famous for.
3. **Education Initiatives**: They funded arts schools and college programs in entertainment management. While the big entertainment companies had their own intense training programs, these schools helped create an environment where pursuing music wasn't seen as just a dream.
4. **Going International**: They created programs to help Korean artists work with international stars. This helped Korean artists learn new styles and make connections worldwide.

While the big entertainment companies (SM, YG, and JYP) did the heavy lifting of creating K-pop stars, the government's support played a big part in allowing Hallyu to thrive. Public support and private innovation, together, turned K-pop into the global powerhouse we know today.

THE KOREAN WAVE BEGINS TO SWELL

In the late '90s and early 2000s, something amazing started happening. All those bold strategies by the Korean government started paying off. Korean culture—not just K-pop, but dramas, movies, and even food—gained traction in neighboring Asian countries.

K-Dramas Lead the Way

Korean TV shows (K-dramas) were the pioneers - they broke through first. These weren't your typical TV shows. With their movie-like quality, addictive storylines, and super charismatic actors, they had people hooked right away.

Imagine walking past an electronics store in Beijing around 2002. The owner's got a TV in the window playing a Korean drama. Before you know it, there's a whole crowd watching, completely invested in the story. In the crowd, there's this girl humming the show's theme song - a K-pop song she got from a copied CD. Similar scenes were unfolding all over Asia.

By 2003, two K-dramas were making history. **Winter Sonata**, a love story of loss and second chances, mesmerized Japan. Middle-aged Japanese women swooned over Bae Yong-joon, the lead actor, affectionately calling him "Yon-sama." Japan's Prime Minister Junichiro Koizumi even joked, "Bae Yong-joon is better known than I am in Japan."

Meanwhile, *Jewel in the Palace* (*Dae Jang Geum*), a historical drama about a royal cook, drew massive viewership in China, Taiwan, and Hong Kong. Its final episode boasted a whopping 47% viewership rating in Hong Kong — nearly half of its population.

These dramas did more than entertain - they gave people their first real look at Korean culture. Viewers fell in love with everything from Korean food to fashion. They wanted to visit Seoul and learn Korean. Later shows got even more creative. Like *My Love from the Star* (about an alien falling for a movie star) and *Descendants of the Sun* (featuring a soldier and doctor falling in love in a war zone) - each one became huge and influenced everything from what people wore to where they wanted to travel.

These K-dramas basically became Korea's unofficial ambassadors, building bridges between countries better than any politician could.

K-pop: The Soundtrack of the Korean Wave

As K-dramas were captivating hearts across Asia, K-pop followed closely behind. Companies like SM, YG, and JYP Entertainment pursued a unique approach: rigorous idol training, Western and Asian pop fusion, and synchronized dance performances. (We will cover these more in detail in later chapters.) The result was a polished product with universal appeal.

In a music store in Tokyo in 2001, one would see teens gathered around a listening station to hear BoA, the first K-pop star to break into Japan's challenging music market. Her Japanese-language songs blew the doors open for K-pop in Japan for future artists to walk through.

K-pop's catchy melodies, dynamic visuals, and charismatic idols appealed across Asia and would do the same, soon enough, around the globe.

THE DIGITAL REVOLUTION: HALLYU 2.0

The late 2000s and early 2010s marked a new chapter in Korean entertainment's world takeover, known as "Hallyu 2.0." This new era was all about how the internet and social media changed the game for Korean pop culture, helping it spread way beyond Asia.

When **YouTube** launched in 2005, it revolutionized how people discovered Korean entertainment. Before, you'd have to catch K-pop music videos on Asian TV channels. But now? Anyone with internet access could watch them anytime, anywhere. This opened up Korean entertainment to entirely new audiences and created worldwide fan communities.

By the mid-2010s, platforms like **Netflix** started featuring Korean content in a major way. They licensed popular K-dramas like *Descendants of the Sun* and even started making their own Korean shows like *Kingdom*. This brought Korean storytelling to viewers who might never have discovered it otherwise.

The "Gangnam Style" Moment

It's 2012, and a teenager in Brazil is scrolling through YouTube. They stumble across PSY's "Gangnam Style" - a music video that would change *everything*. With its catchy tune, quirky dance, and colorful visuals, it became the first YouTube video to hit a billion views. This wasn't just a viral video; it was K-pop's introduction to millions of new fans worldwide.

The Power of Digital

This was Hallyu 2.0 - Korean entertainment's second wave, powered by the internet. Korean content was now just a click away for anyone interested. K-pop groups built international fan bases, K-dramas found viewers far beyond Asia, and Korean variety shows like *Running Man* became must-watch content globally. What started as regional success in Asia had transformed into a worldwide cultural phenomenon.

THE HALLYU EFFECT BEYOND ENTERTAINMENT

The Korean Wave extended far beyond entertainment, transforming South Korea's economy, diplomacy, and cultural influence.

The Economic Impact

By 2019, South Korea's cultural exports reached around $12.3 billion. Hallyu boosted industries like tourism, fashion, and cosmetics. Right before the pandemic, Seoul's shopping districts were packed with tourists from everywhere, eager to experience the world of K-dramas and K-pop firsthand, buying Korean skincare products, clothes, and K-pop albums. They weren't just buying products; they were taking home pieces of Korean culture.

Beauty and Fashion Take Off

Korean beauty products (K-beauty) have become huge worldwide. Korean fashion also blew up, especially when K-pop stars and K-drama actors wore certain brands. These celebrities became so influential that major luxury fashion brands wanted them as representatives. When they walked through airports or appeared on red carpets, whatever they wore would often sell out instantly.

International Relations and Influence

Korean pop culture did something remarkable - it completely changed how the world sees South Korea. Even world leaders like Barack Obama and Emmanuel Macron have talked about how influential Korean culture has become. South Korea transformed its image from a war-torn country to a global trendsetter.

Once the government saw how powerful K-pop could be in international relations, it started using it smartly. Korean embassies began organizing K-pop events worldwide to build friendships with other countries. At a Korea-China friendship concert in Shanghai, fans from both countries would come together because they love the same music. These events did more than entertain - they helped ease tensions between countries and opened new markets for Korean products.

Language Learning Boom

As Korean entertainment spread globally, more people wanted to learn Korean. Between 2010 and 2018, the number of Korean language students worldwide grew dramatically. Many fans wanted to understand their favorite songs and shows without relying on subtitles. Organizations like the King Sejong Institute, which promotes Korean education, expanded to meet this growing demand.

This interest in the language went deeper - many fans started learning about Korea's history and traditions, too. Learning Korean became a way for fans to connect more deeply with the culture they'd fallen in love with through K-pop and K-dramas.

THE WAVE REACHES NEW HEIGHTS

Hallyu's impact continued to grow, breaking new ground. In 2020, *Parasite* made history as the first non-English language film to win the Academy Award for Best Picture. Director Bong Joon-ho's film wasn't just entertaining - it was a brilliant mix of dark humor and social commentary that made audiences everywhere think. It showed that Korean filmmaking could compete with and even surpass Hollywood's best.

Then came 2021's *Squid Game* on Netflix, which became one of the most-watched shows in the world. This intense drama about desperate people playing deadly versions of children's games for money struck a chord with viewers everywhere. More than just thrilling entertainment, it got people talking about serious issues like economic inequality and the darker sides of capitalism.

These successes proved something important: Korean entertainment had evolved beyond just being popular - it was now shaping global conversations and winning the highest honors in entertainment. What started as a local entertainment industry had grown into a creative powerhouse that could influence how people around the world think and feel about important issues.

Fun Fact: The finger heart—formed by crossing the thumb and index finger— was popularized by K-drama and K-pop stars as a cute way to show love. It began in South Korea around the early 2010s, quickly becoming a global symbol of affection and the Korean Wave.

CHALLENGES AND CONTROVERSIES: THE DARK UNDERCURRENTS OF THE KOREAN WAVE

As the Korean Wave swept across the globe, it didn't just bring catchy tunes and heartwarming dramas. Like any powerful current, it also stirred up turbulent waters, facing challenges and controversies that threatened to dampen its momentum. Let's explore the less glamorous side of Hallyu.

The Backlash: When the Wave Hits a Wall

Imagine you're in a bustling Beijing street in 2016. Everywhere you look, there are advertisements featuring Korean celebrities, stores selling K-beauty products, and cafes playing K-pop hits. But suddenly, the music stops. The posters come down. The Korean Wave, it seems, has hit a Great Wall.

This scene played out in reality when China, once a massive market for Korean entertainment, imposed unofficial sanctions on Korean cultural imports starting in 2016. The reason? **Political tensions** over South Korea's deployment of a U.S. missile defense system, THAAD. Overnight, K-pop concerts were canceled, K-dramas disappeared from streaming platforms, and even Korean celebrities' social media accounts went dark in China.

But China wasn't the only country to push back. In Japan, anti-Korean sentiment, often rooted in **historical grievances**, has sometimes led to protests against the Korean Wave. Some Japanese nationalists have decried the "invasion" of Korean culture, seeing it as a threat to their own cultural identity. But while political tensions, such as disputes over historical issues or territorial claims, have strained relations, K-pop and K-dramas have continued to maintain a substantial fanbase in Japan, demonstrating the resilience of cultural exchange even amidst political friction.

These backlashes serve as a stark reminder that culture, no matter how popular, is never entirely separate from politics and history. The Korean Wave, for all its soft power, sometimes found itself caught in the cross-currents of international relations.

Cultural Crosscurrents: The Appropriation Debate

As Korean popular culture ventured further into global waters, it encountered another storm: accusations of cultural appropriation. Think about a music video where K-pop idols sport cornrows and gold chains, echoing African American hip-hop aesthetics, or a K-drama where characters casually use sacred symbols from other cultures as fashion accessories.

These instances have sparked heated debates about **cultural sensitivity and authenticity**. Critics argue that Korean entertainment sometimes borrows elements from other cultures without proper understanding or respect. Defenders counter that this is part of the global cultural exchange that K-pop and K-dramas encourage.

This controversy highlights the complex navigation required as the Korean Wave interacts with diverse global cultures. It's a reminder that with great influence comes great responsibility—and the need for cultural awareness and respect.

Industry Pressures: The Hidden Cost of Success

Behind the perfect performances and catchy songs, there's a tougher reality. The Korean entertainment industry, especially K-pop, has faced criticism over its intense training system and the pressure it puts on young performers. While this system creates incredibly skilled artists, people have raised serious concerns about the **mental and physical health** of these young performers.

Several tragic incidents in recent years have started important conversations about mental health and fair treatment in the industry. As Korean entertainment continues to grow globally, many are asking: Is the human cost of this success too high?

(We'll look more closely at these K-pop industry issues in upcoming chapters.)

THE FUTURE OF HALLYU

As we look to the future, the Korean Wave shows no signs of receding. From K-dramas and K-pop to webtoons and video games, Korean creative content continues to find new audiences and push boundaries.

The Korean government continues to support this cultural expansion as a key part of its economic strategy, even launching special programs like "Visit Korea Year 2023-2024" to welcome tourists back after the pandemic — especially fans eager to experience the home of their favorite entertainers.

. . .

FROM ITS HUMBLE beginnings in the late 1990s and 2000s, as a way to recover from the Asian Financial Crisis, to its current status as a global cultural powerhouse, the story of Hallyu is one of innovation, perseverance, and the universal appeal of well-crafted entertainment. This wave has not only transformed the entertainment landscape but has also reshaped how South Korea is seen on the world stage.

With this strong foundation in place, K-pop artists are poised to make even bigger waves on the global stage. Their stories - which we'll explore in upcoming chapters - show just how far Korean entertainment has come and hint at where it might go next.

CHAPTER 4

THE K-POP MACHINE
INSIDE THE IDOL-MAKING SYSTEM

WE'VE MENTIONED the K-pop training system several times already - how entertainment companies scout and develop talent, and how they've turned creating pop stars into almost a science. But it is such a crucial part of understanding K-pop's global success that it deserves its own chapter.

When people call it the "K-pop manufacturing machine," they're not far from the truth. It is a well-coordinated process that combines finding raw talent, years of intense training, and smart marketing strategies. This system has created some of the most skilled performers in pop music today — artists who can sing, dance, rap, and entertain with seemingly effortless precision.

Of course, the concept of management-assembled music groups is nothing new. This approach has a long history in the U.S., dating back to the 1960s with acts like The Monkees and continuing into the 1990s with groups such as *NSYNC and the Backstreet Boys; and let's not forget the British contributions to this trend including the Spice Girls in the 1990s and One Direction in the 2010s.

While these groups achieved massive popularity, their "manufactured" origins were often scoffed at as something artificial or inauthentic. In K-pop, however, the process of forming groups through entertainment companies is openly celebrated, becoming a core part of the industry's identity and charm.

In this chapter, we'll pull back the curtain and look at how this system works - from how it started to how it is still shaping pop music today. Whether you think this system is brilliant or objectionable (and many people think it's both), understanding it is key to understanding K-pop's worldwide success.

THE BIRTH OF A REVOLUTION

To understand the K-pop machine, we need to travel back to the mid-1990s, in the wake of Seo Taiji and Boys' industry-shaking success. Picture a small, cluttered office in Seoul, circa 1995. Sitting at a desk piled high with papers and demo tapes was **Lee Soo-man**, a former folk singer with a vision. He had just founded SM Entertainment, and he was about to change the Korean music industry forever.

While studying in America, Lee was inspired by how companies like Motown developed their artists. But he didn't just want to copy their approach - he wanted to make it better. Instead of just finding talented singers or dancers, he imagined creating complete performers through intensive training. He called this system **"cultural technology"** - a methodical way to develop and promote artists.

As Lee established SM Entertainment, two other visionaries were hatching their own plans. When Seo Taiji and Boys disbanded in 1996, **Yang Hyun-suk**, one of its members, founded YG Entertainment. His vision was different - he wanted to create artists with a more rebellious, hip-hop style. YG became known for performers with attitude and edge.

In 1997, **Park Jin-young**, a successful solo artist, launched JYP Entertainment. Park's philosophy emphasized musicality and personal growth, nurturing artists who were not just polished performers but genuine musicians. He focused on developing the personal and creative sides of his trainees, aiming to build well-rounded artists with a strong sense of individuality.

These three companies—SM, YG, and JYP—soon became known as the **"Big Three."** They shaped the K-pop industry for decades to come, each with its own distinct style and approach, creating a new generation of stars who would set the stage for K-pop's rise to global prominence.

Fun Fact: In the early 80s, after leaving his singing career, Lee Soo-man went to study computer engineering at California State University at Northridge, where he witnessed the rise of "superstars of the MTV generation" such as Michael Jackson.

HOW THE SYSTEM WORKS

So, how exactly does the Idol-making process work? In some cases, talents are scouted off the street by agency talent scouts, but most spend years preparing and honing their skills, and all of them must go through...

The Audition: Where Dreams Begin... or End

The first step in the K-pop idol-making process is the audition. While Lee Soo-man drew some inspiration from the American entertainment industry, it was the Japanese idol industry—particularly the training methods of Johnny Kitagawa—that directly influenced the creation of the K-pop trainee system. Lee adapted this model for Korea.

Today, thousands of hopefuls around the globe attend auditions held by Korean entertainment agencies every year. While auditions are still mainly held in Korea, they have increasingly been held in cities around the world—places like New York, Tokyo, and Bangkok—reflecting K-pop's growing global reach.

Let's paint a picture of what these auditions look like. It's a crisp autumn morning in Seoul, circa 2005. The streets are buzzing with energy as hundreds of young hopefuls line up outside a nondescript building. Some have been camping out since the night before, clutching registration forms and bottled water. There's a palpable mix of excitement and nervousness in the air.

Among the crowd, we might spot a young girl, let's call her Min-seo. She's 14, bright-eyed and full of dreams. She's been practicing BoA's song "No. 1" for months, hoping this could be her big break. As she waits, she chats with the boy next to her in line, Jae-hoon, who's here to show off his dance moves. They share stories of their favorite idols, of watching *Music Bank* every Friday, and of dreaming about standing on that same stage one day.

Inside the audition hall, the atmosphere is electric. Starry-eyed hopefuls are everywhere, practicing their routines in corners, warming up their voices, stretching their limbs, or just sitting quietly, lost in thought. When their numbers are called, they step into small rooms where panels of judges await with their faces impassive.

The judges are looking not just for polished skills, but for potential. Someone who comes in as a dancer might be molded into a vocalist later, or vice versa. The agencies are looking for raw materials they can shape and refine. This is part of what makes the K-pop system unique—its ability to see potential and craft it into stardom.

Fun Fact: Many hopefuls audition for multiple agencies several times; while the number of auditions varies greatly, persistence is often key to breaking into the industry. IU (Lee Ji-eun) is reputed to have gone through the most auditions in K-pop — 20, before she debuted.

THE TRAINEE LIFE: A BALANCING ACT OF DREAMS, EDUCATION, AND RIGOROUS TRAINING

Those who make it through auditions enter the next phase: Life as a K-pop trainee. This journey demands an incredible balance of rigorous training, academic work, and personal sacrifice.

Imagine Min-seo's day as a trainee. Her alarm goes off at 5:30 a.m., jolting her awake in the dormitory she shares with three other trainees. By 6:00 a.m., she's at her first vocal lesson. Her trainer pushes her hard, and by 7:00 a.m., she's heading to her middle school, still mentally revisiting the notes she struggled with in the morning. In South Korea, education isn't just important - it's everything. The country takes enormous pride in having one of the world's highest high school graduation rates, over 95%.

From morning until early afternoon, Min-seo tries to be just another student, dealing with tests and friend drama like anyone else. But while her classmates head to after-school tutoring, her other life calls. After a full school day, she races back to the agency's building, changing clothes on the way. Dance practice begins at 4:00 p.m. Here, we find Jae-hoon as well, learning new choreography with military precision. The trainer isn't satisfied—"Sharper, cleaner!"—so they try again. The evening continues with singing practice, language lessons in Japanese or English, and training in variety show skills - because modern K-pop stars need to be entertainers, not just singers. They need to know how to handle interviews, work with fans, and shine on camera.

By the time Min-seo gets back to her dorm at 10:00 PM, she still has homework waiting. The pressure to keep up good grades never lets up. Often, it's past midnight before she finally rests, knowing another day of the same intensity waits just a few hours away.

Balancing Training and Education

The pressure comes from all sides. Trainees must regularly perform for company executives who decide their fate - one bad evaluation could end the dream. Meanwhile, they can't let their grades slip. Some companies work with schools that understand the trainees' schedules, but many trainees attend regular schools, somehow making it all work.

As trainees get older and closer to debut, they might choose different paths for school:

- Some transfer to arts high schools with more flexible schedules
- Others switch to online classes
- Some work with private tutors who can teach around their training

Even after K-pop stars debut, many keep studying beyond high school. They enroll in university courses and chase degrees through online programs or with special arrangements. This isn't just about respecting education - it's also practical. Even successful K-pop careers often end while the stars are still young, and having an education means having options.

Fun Facts: The training period for a K-pop trainee can range from months to years, but the average is said to be 2-4 years. Jimin of BTS trained for about 8-10 months at Big Hit Entertainment before debuting. The members of BLACK-PINK spent 4 to 6 years in training. G.Soul, a solo artist, spent 15 years as a JYP trainee before his debut. G-Dragon of BIGBANG trained for about 5 years under SM Entertainment as a child and another 6 years at YG Entertainment, totaling roughly 11 years before his debut.

THE AGENCY: ARCHITECTS OF IDOLS

While the trainees work tirelessly, the agencies are equally busy, shaping the concept of what a K-pop idol should be. Each of the Big Three agencies touts its own approach:

1. **SM Entertainment** focuses on creating polished idol groups with an emphasis on vocal and dance proficiency. Known for its state-of-the-art facilities and rigorous training, SM is sometimes seen as a "factory" for its highly structured approach.
2. **YG Entertainment** emphasizes individual artistry and self-expression, encouraging trainees to explore their own musical styles. This has led to innovative acts, especially in hip-hop and R&B. YG artists often stand out with their distinctive, authentic style.
3. **JYP Entertainment** aims for a balance, focusing on both professional skills and personal growth. Park Jin-young's involvement in the training process varies but often includes imparting life lessons. This approach has produced relatable, well-rounded idols.

These agencies plan every aspect of an idol's career, from music style to fashion concepts, and individual roles. Each piece is carefully designed to create acts that are more than the sum of their parts.

Fun Fact: Each of the Big Three is estimated to have between 20-60 trainees at a time, though the numbers vary. Smaller agencies tend to have fewer.

Other Agencies

While SM, YG, and JYP have long dominated, others like **HYBE Labels** (formerly **Big Hit Entertainment**) have made significant impacts. Founded by Bang Si-hyuk in 2005, HYBE rose to prominence with BTS's debut in 2013. Today, it operates as a multi-label conglomerate, housing labels like **Big Hit Music, Pledis Entertainment**, and **Source Music.**

DSP Media, founded in 1991, played a significant role in the first generation of K-pop with Sechs Kies and Fin.K.L. It later produced successful acts like KARA, focusing on Japan promotions.

Cube Entertainment, established in 2006 by former JYP employees, has produced groups like BEAST (now Highlight), 4Minute, and (G)I-DLE, offering some creative freedom in music production.

FNC Entertainment, known for its focus on band-oriented acts like CNBLUE and FT Island, also created successful idol groups like AOA and SF9.

Starship Entertainment has grown steadily with acts like SISTAR, MONSTA X, and IVE, known for producing vocally strong groups.

Other influential agencies like **Pledis Entertainment** (now part of HYBE), **RBW**, and **Jellyfish Entertainment** add to the diversity of K-pop, each contributing with their unique styles and training philosophies.

DEBUT: THE DREAM REALIZED

After years of training, the moment every trainee dreams of finally arrives: debut. He or she has been selected by the company to be either a member of a group or a solo artist. But this is just the beginning. In the weeks and months following their debut, new idols' lives become a whirlwind of performances, fan meetings, and variety show appearances.

The pressure, if anything, is even more intense than during their trainee days. Every performance is scrutinized by fans and critics alike. They need to be perfect on stage, charming off stage, and always mindful of their image.

Their agency continues to play a huge role in their lives. Every schedule, every appearance, and every social media post is carefully managed. They're no longer just trainees or employees but valuable company assets representing the agency's brand. Many idols continue to live in company-provided housing or dormitories even after their debut, allowing for easier coordination of their busy schedules.

Fun Fact: Estimates suggest that less than 10% of trainees actually make it to debut. Each year, around 100 groups debut in South Korea, but less than 5% of them survive beyond their initial years due to the intense competition.

THE DARK SIDE OF THE DREAM

No discussion of the K-pop industry would be complete without acknowledging its darker aspects. The intense pressure placed on young trainees and idols has raised serious concerns about **mental health and well-being**.

The level of control exerted by agencies has also been a point of contention. The term **"slave contracts"** has often been used to describe contracts with unfair terms, especially in the 2000s and early 2010s, due to their restrictive nature and lengthy durations.

While reforms by the Korea Fair Trade Commission (KFTC) have improved conditions, some idols continue to face challenges regarding profit distribution and contract terms. A director from DSP Media once noted that while the company shares profits with performers, significant costs often leave little for the artists themselves, highlighting the financial realities of the industry, where even successful idols may not be reaping significant financial rewards.

Fun Fact: The "Seventh Year Itch" in K-pop refers to the pivotal point when idol groups often face big decisions due to expiring contracts, typically set at seven years. Around this time, groups might renew their contracts, some members may pursue solo careers, or—much to fans' dismay—groups may disband entirely.

Another concern is **the emphasis on physical appearance**, which has been criticized for promoting unrealistic beauty standards. While some trainees have reported being encouraged to undergo **plastic surgeries** like blepharoplasty (eyelid surgery) or rhinoplasty ("nose job") to align with Korean beauty standards, the extent of such requirements varies by agency.

Idols also face challenges in their personal lives, including **dating bans**. Many companies implement policies that restrict dating, especially in the early years of an idol's career, to preserve an illusion of availability to fans. While the strictness of these bans has lessened in recent years, the notion that dating could harm an idol's image remains strong.

THE FINANCIAL SIDE OF K-POP: WHO REALLY BENEFITS?

The K-pop industry's financial structure is complicated and often misunderstood. At first glance, it might look like all involved—from agencies to idols—are automatically millionaires. But a closer look reveals a more complex picture.

The Agency-Trainee Relationship

At the heart of the K-pop financial system lies the relationship between entertainment agencies and their trainees and idols. As we explored earlier, this relationship is based on contracts that have historically favored the agencies. Two key factors are at work:

Trainee Debt: Traditionally, trainees had to repay their agencies for all costs during training: singing and dancing lessons, outfits, housing, meals, and more. After public criticism and new regulations, bigger companies like HYBE now often cover these costs themselves.

However, smaller agencies still make trainees pay everything back, creating a significant gap between trainees at major and minor agencies.

Profit Sharing: Even after debut, most idols don't get rich right away. They first have to pay off their training costs, which means even seemingly successful groups may have to perform for years before seeing real money. While contracts are getting fairer over time, entertainment agencies still keep most of the revenue, especially in the beginning years of an idol's career.

The Price Tag of Creating an Idol

Creating a K-pop star isn't cheap. According to some estimates, companies spend between $100,000 to $500,000 to turn a regular teenager into an idol – that's the price of a house in many places. This money goes into:

- Years of dance and vocal training
- Housing and food for trainees
- Everything needed for debut (outfits, music videos, promotion)
- Creating the perfect idol image

The spending does not end with the debut. Companies continue to invest a lot of money into promoting and protecting their assets. For groups meant to compete internationally, like BTS or BLACKPINK, companies spend even more.

Fun Fact: In 2012, The Wall Street Journal reported that the cost of training a single K-pop idol under SM Entertainment averaged $3 million — including expenses such as vocal and dance training, housing, wardrobe, and promotional activities.

The Reality of Idol Earnings

So, how much do K-pop idols make? The answer is, of course, "depends." It varies dramatically based on their level of success and agency affiliation.

- **Average Earnings:** According to the South Korean National Tax Service, the average annual earnings for a Korean idol in 2013 were approximately US$42,000, up from US$25,275 in 2010, thanks to the global spread of K-pop. But these averages don't tell the whole story.

- **Top-Tier Idols:** Once debts are repaid, idols from major agencies who achieve mainstream success can earn millions annually, especially through endorsements, brand deals, and international activities. Their earnings often extend far beyond music sales and performances.
- **Mid-Tier and Struggling Idols:** Most idols earn far less, sometimes struggling financially even after debut. Those from smaller agencies often face the highest burdens, with limited income and fewer opportunities for lucrative activities.

THE EVOLUTION OF THE SYSTEM AND ITS IMPACT

As K-pop has grown, so too has the training system. New agencies have emerged, each putting their own spin on the formula established by the Big Three. Some have experimented with more transparent training processes, even turning the experience into reality TV shows like *Produce 101* and *Sixteen*. These shows have given fans a glimpse into the trainee world and a say in which trainees debut, adding a new layer of audience engagement to the idol creation process — though they have faced criticism for vote manipulation and lack of transparency.

The globalization of K-pop has brought further changes. Training idols in foreign languages, particularly English, Japanese, and Chinese, has become increasingly important. Many agencies also actively recruit international trainees, aiming to create groups with global appeal.

Despite the criticisms and challenges, there's no denying the impact this system has had on K-pop's global success. The intense training regime produces performers with exceptional skill and versatility, creating acts that are more than just musicians—they are all-around entertainers.

Also, the system's emphasis on constant improvement and adaptation has kept K-pop evolving. This adaptability has allowed it to stay fresh and relevant, continually attracting new fans around the world.

As WE CONTINUE our journey into K-pop's rise, remember Min-seo and Jae-hoon—two young dreamers who represent the countless trainees working to turn their passion into reality. The K-pop machine may be demanding, but for those who succeed, it can transform dreams into worldwide fame, making it well worth the price of sacrifice and hard work.

CHAPTER 5

THE EVOLUTION OF K-POP
THE GOLDEN AGE OF SECOND-GENERATION K-POP STARS: 2003-2011

JUST LIKE HOW we talk about millennials and Gen Z, K-pop has its own "generations." Each one lasts about 5-7 years and has its own special flavor – unique music styles, fashion trends, and ways of doing things. Fans came up with this idea in the late 2000s as a way to categorize idols and groups based on their debut year and shared impact.

It's a useful shorthand for discussing K-pop's history and the waves of artists who've shaped it over time. The generally accepted classification (by year of debut) is as follows:

- **First Generation (1997-2002):** The pioneers
- **Second Generation (2003-2011):** K-pop goes regional
- **Third Generation (2012-2017):** The global breakthrough
- **Fourth Generation (2018-2022):** Digital domination
- **Fifth Generation (2023-):** Just getting started

But keep in mind, this is not an exact science—boundaries between generations can be fuzzy. Many artists don't fit perfectly into one generation, and there's often debate about where one generation ends and another begins. So consider it more of a helpful guide than a strict rule book.

Fun Fact: PSY, of Gangnam Style *fame, is a good example of a hard-to-classify artist. Technically, he is a 1st Generation artist, given that he first debuted in*

2001. However, he re-signed with YG in 2010 and shot to global stardom with
his mega-hit in 2012, so many consider him a 3rd Generation artist.

THE SECOND GENERATION STEPS UP: A NEW ERA BEGINS

As the new millennium dawned, South Korea was rising from the ashes
of the 1997 financial crisis. The early 2000s ushered in a period of
economic resurgence and cultural renaissance. Hallyu was in full swing.
This era, spanning roughly from 2003 to 2011, saw a new wave of K-pop
stars emerge who would completely change the game and eventually
help K-pop take over playlists worldwide.

The Perfect Storm: Three Forces Behind the Rise

1. **Economic Growth** — South Korea's economy soared in the
   2000s, with its GDP doubling from $504 billion to over $1 trillion
   in just a decade. This financial strength gave entertainment
   companies the resources to develop more ambitious projects and
   invest heavily in artist development.
2. **Digital Revolution** — The nation was in the midst of a digital
   revolution. The rapid spread of technology changed everything:
   - *High-speed internet* spread rapidly across the country; by
     2010, nearly 95% of South Korean households had broadband
     access. This widespread connectivity made instant music
     distribution and more immediate online fan engagement
     possible.
   - As K-pop began to gain momentum, the *smartphone boom*
     arrived just in time. The introduction of the iPhone in 2009
     and Samsung's Galaxy series in 2010 transformed how fans
     consumed content. Now, they can carry K-pop in their
     pockets!
   - *Streaming platforms and social media* made K-pop instantly
     accessible worldwide making music videos, dance practices,
     and behind-the-scenes content available anytime, anywhere.
3. **Strategic Government Support** — Recognizing its benefits, the
   South Korean government amplified its support for the Korean
   Wave (Hallyu), including not just K-pop but also K-dramas,
   films, and other cultural exports. What began as modest cultural
   promotion efforts in 1999 soon saw a significant boost in funding
   —from around $74 million in 2001 to over $180 million by 2009.

This combination of economic strength, technological advancement, and government backing created the perfect conditions for K-pop's transformation from a local industry into a global cultural force.

DEFINING FEATURES & INDUSTRY INNOVATIONS: WHAT MADE SECOND-GENERATION IDOLS SPECIAL

The second generation of K-pop marked a transformative era in the industry, characterized by several key developments:

Intensified Training: The already rigorous training process became even more demanding. While training durations varied, many aspiring idols now spent 2-4 years, and in some cases up to 5-7 years, honing their skills. This created a new standard for performers who excelled at singing, dancing, and entertainment.

Global Expansion: K-pop's ambitions extended beyond Korean shores, leading to a surge in cultural content exports. The value of these exports, which included K-pop alongside TV dramas and films, grew from around $13.9 million in 2005 to approximately $83.2 million by 2010.

Performance-Centric Approach: Dance and performance skills became central to an idol's appeal. Dance practice videos gained popularity, offering fans a glimpse into the hard work behind polished performances. For example, 2PM's "Again & Again" dance practice video attracted a lot of attention in 2009, highlighting the power of raw, behind-the-scenes content.

Point Choreography: Memorable, easy-to-recognize dance moves became crucial for creating viral appeal. Brown Eyed Girls' "Abracadabra" hip dance is a prime example of this trend, setting a precedent for signature moves that could quickly spread across fan communities.

Concept Flexibility: Groups began reinventing their image and sound with each "comeback" (new release), keeping fans engaged and showcasing their versatility — from powerful to cute to sophisticated. This approach allowed idols to keep up with changing musical trends and audience preferences.

Diverse Group Makeup: The inclusion of non-Korean members became more common, reflecting K-pop's aim to appeal to broader markets. Notable examples include Nichkhun from Thailand in 2PM and Victoria from China in f(x), who helped bridge cultural gaps and attract international fans.

Reality Show Exposure: Programs like *We Got Married* and *Invincible Youth* allowed fans to see idols' personalities beyond the stage, fostering deeper emotional connections. These shows provided a new way for fans to engage with idols, strengthening their loyalty and admiration.

Digital Singles: As digital platforms rose in popularity, idols began releasing more singles between full albums. This allowed for more frequent, constant engagement with fans.

Powerful Fandoms: Perhaps most significantly, this period saw the rise of intensely dedicated fan cultures. Official fan clubs swelled in size, with TVXQ's "Cassiopeia" boasting around 800,000 members by 2008. These passionate communities became the backbone of K-pop's global spread, leveraging social media and online platforms to promote their favorite artists beyond South Korea's borders.

NOTABLE SECOND-GENERATION K-POP IDOLS AND THEIR IMPACTS

Let's explore the iconic groups, groundbreaking songs, and industry innovations that defined the second generation of K-pop and set the stage for its eventual global conquest.

TVXQ (2003-Present, SM Ent.): Pioneers of K-pop's expansion into Japan, TVXQ set numerous records throughout their career. Their debut single, "Hug," was well-received, and "Rising Sun" (2005) showcased intricate choreography. In 2009, they became one of the first K-pop groups to perform at the Tokyo Dome, selling out 50,000 seats. Their fan club, Cassiopeia, became a cultural phenomenon in its own right. Despite a major lineup change in 2009, with members Jaejoong, Yoochun, and Junsu forming JYJ, TVXQ's impact remained significant. *Mirotic* (2008) sold over 600,000 copies, making it one of the highest-selling albums of the 2000s.

Lee Hyori (solo, 2003-Present, DSP, Mnet Media, etc.): Formerly of Fin.K.L, Lee Hyori emerged as a solo sensation known for her charisma and bold stage presence. She pushed boundaries in the industry, challenging conservative norms with her confident image and becoming a role model for future female soloists.

Se7en (solo, 2003-Present, YG Ent.): A pioneer of male solo idols, Se7en gained fame with R&B hits like "Come Back to Me" (2003) and expanded his reach with the Japanese single "Hikari" and the U.S. release "Girls" (2009), demonstrating K-pop's global ambitions.

Super Junior (2005-Present, SM Ent.): Known for their large member count and sub-unit strategy, Super Junior debuted with 12 members, later expanding to 13 with the addition of Kyuhyun in 2006. Their hit "Sorry, Sorry" (2009), with its catchy point choreo became a viral sensation across Asia, inspiring dance covers worldwide. They were also known for their various sub-units, including Super Junior-M, which targeted the Chinese market, and members like Heechul became variety show mainstays.

SS501 (2005-2010, DSP Media): One of the early K-pop groups to find a foothold in Japan alongside TVXQ. Leader Kim Hyun-joong's role in the hit drama *Boys Over Flowers* (2009) gave the group a boost in popularity. The music video for their song "Love Ya" (2010) was known for its high production value.

BIGBANG (2006-Present, YG Ent.): BIGBANG revolutionized K-pop with their hip-hop sound and self-produced music, setting them apart as one of the most influential acts of the second generation. "Lies" (2007) dominated digital charts for eight consecutive weeks, cementing their place in K-pop history. G-Dragon and T.O.P's background as underground rappers helped shape the group's distinct style, which also left a lasting impact on fashion trends in Korea.

Brown Eyed Girls (2006-Present, Nega/APOP): Known for avoiding the "cute" concepts typical of many girl groups, Brown Eyed Girls embraced mature themes. Their song "Abracadabra" (2009) popularized the "arrogant dance," influencing many subsequent K-pop choreographies. Ga-In's solo career further pushed boundaries with its provocative themes.

Wonder Girls (2007-2017, JYP Ent.): Pioneers in K-pop's early foray into the U.S. market, their song "Nobody" (2008) made them the first K-pop act to chart on the Billboard Hot 100, peaking at #76. Their retro-themed hits, including "Tell Me" (2007), created dance crazes across Korea. They later transitioned to a band concept in 2015, a bold shift that highlighted their versatility.

Girls' Generation (2007-Present, SM Ent.): Synonymous with the rise of K-pop girl groups, Girls' Generation set new standards with their synchronized performances and trendsetting style. "Gee" (2009) topped KBS Music Bank for nine consecutive weeks and sparked a fashion trend with its colorful "skinny jeans." Their success in Japan, with their first Japanese album selling over 500,000 copies, helped expand K-pop's reach overseas.

F.T. Island (2007-Present, FNC Ent.): As one of K-pop's first idol bands in which members played their own instruments, F.T. Island gained attention with their debut song "Love Sick" and achieved significant popularity in Japan. Leader Lee Hong-gi's distinctive vocals and acting roles helped solidify their reputation.

KARA (2007-2016, DSP Media): After a rocky start, KARA rebranded with a cuter image through "Rock U" (2008) and gained international success with the "butt dance" from "Mister" (2009). They found major success in Japan, with "Mister" becoming a significant hit, selling hundreds of thousands of copies. They adapted to lineup changes through public auditions, showing their resilience.

IU (solo, 2008-Present, LOEN Ent.): Debuting at 15, IU rose to prominence with "Good Day" (2010), known for its impressive three-octave high note. She transitioned from a youthful image to a mature artist, becoming one of Korea's most respected soloists. Her acting roles in dramas like *Dream High* (2011) and *Hotel Del Luna* (2019) cemented her as a versatile star.

SHINee (2008-Present, SM Ent.): Known for their polished live performances and trendsetting fashion, SHINee debuted with "Replay" (2008), which popularized the "Noona Fan" (older female fan) trend. Member Jonghyun's contributions to songwriting added depth to their music, while Taemin's later solo career showcased his remarkable dance skills.

2PM (2008-Present, JYP Ent.): Embracing an athletic, "beast idol" concept, 2PM stood out with acrobatic performances in songs like "10 Out of 10" (2008). The departure of Jay Park in 2009 created controversy, but the group rebounded with "Heartbeat" (2009), which featured high production values and marked a turning point in their career.

Taeyang (solo, 2008-Present, YG Ent.): A member of BIGBANG, Taeyang gained acclaim for his R&B style, particularly through solo hits like "Only Look at Me" (2008) and "Wedding Dress" (2009), which became a favorite for international fans on YouTube.

SECRET (2009-2018, TS Ent.): Known for their versatility, SECRET captured audiences with hits like "Magic" and "Shy Boy," seamlessly shifting between sultry and retro-cute concepts. Their strong domestic presence and memorable performances made them a standout girl group of the second generation.

ZE:A (2009-2017, Star Empire Ent.): Though ZE:A's group success was modest, their hits like "Mazeltov" and "Aftermath" showcased their versatility. Members like Siwan and Hyungsik later achieved fame in acting, extending the group's influence beyond music.

T-ara (2009-2017, MBK Ent.): T-ara rose to fame with catchy hits like "Bo Peep Bo Peep" (2009) and "Roly-Poly" (2011). Hugely popular in China, they became a leading example of K-pop's international appeal, even as false bullying accusations briefly impacted their reputation.

2NE1 (2009-2016, YG Ent.): 2NE1 shattered traditional girl group norms with their powerful style and bold fashion. Their debut, "Fire," featured two distinct music videos, and "I Am the Best" (2011) became a global anthem, winning Song of the Year at the Mnet Asian Music Awards.

4Minute (2009-2016, Cube Ent.): With their debut, "Hot Issue," 4Minute introduced a confident image that contrasted with more traditional concepts. Their video for "Volume Up" (2012) was notable for its overseas production.

G-Dragon (solo, 2009-Present, YG Ent.): BIGBANG's leader, G-Dragon, made a splash with his solo debut "Heartbreaker" (2009), which sold over 200,000 copies. His influence extended beyond music, as his trendsetting fashion and self-produced work helped shape modern K-pop.

Fun Fact: G-Dragon, the leader of BigBang, was the first K-pop artist to sign an exclusive ambassador contract with a European luxury fashion house when Chanel offered him the role in 2016.

BEAST/Highlight (2009-Present, Cube Ent./Around Us Ent.): Originally named "B2ST," they quickly rebranded before debuting. Known for songs like "Fiction" (2011), BEAST showed the challenges of rebranding when they left Cube Entertainment and renamed themselves Highlight in 2017.

f(x) (2009-2019, SM Ent.): Renowned for their experimental sound, f(x) gained critical acclaim for albums like "Pink Tape" (2013). Amber's androgynous style challenged gender norms, and Victoria's success in China expanded the group's reach.

After School (2009-2019, Pledis Ent.): Known for their "graduation" system — where the member line-up changed fairly regularly, After School set themselves apart by showcasing unique performance skills like drumming and tap dancing. Their sub-unit Orange Caramel gained popularity with quirky hits like "Catallena" (2014).

CNBLUE (2009-Present, FNC Ent.): One of the few idol bands playing instruments, CNBLUE reversed the usual K-pop strategy by debuting in Japan first. "I'm a Loner" (2010) made them a breakout success in Korea, with leader Jung Yong-hwa becoming known for his songwriting abilities.

HyunA (solo, 2010-Present, Cube Ent.): After stints in Wonder Girls and 4Minute, HyunA made waves as a solo artist with "Change" and "Bubble Pop!" (2011), embracing a bold, sexy image that set her apart in the industry.

SISTAR (2010-2017, Starship Ent.): Known as the "summer queens," SISTAR's catchy hits like "Touch My Body" (2014) became seasonal staples. Their amicable disbandment in 2017 was seen as a positive example in the industry.

Miss A (2010-2017, JYP Ent.): Debuting with the hit "Bad Girl Good Girl," Miss A quickly made their mark. Member Suzy's rise as the "Nation's First Love" through acting roles brought extra attention to the group.

INFINITE (2010-Present, Woolim Ent.): Known for their precise synchronization, INFINITE made waves with their "scorpion dance" in "Before the Dawn" (2011). "The Chaser" (2012) was named the best K-pop song of the year by *Billboard*, solidifying their reputation for excellence.

TEEN TOP (2010-Present, TOP Media): Renowned for their synchronized choreography and viral tracks like "Clap" and "No More Perfume on You," TEEN TOP embodied youthful energy. Their polished dance performances set a standard for precision in K-pop stages.

Apink (2011-Present, IST Ent.): Apink gained fame with their "pure" concept and hits like "No No No" (2013) and "LUV" (2014). Their seamless transition to mature styles, as seen in "%% (Eung Eung)" (2019), solidified their status as one of K-pop's longest-running and most influential girl groups.

LEGACY OF INFLUENCE AND IMPACT

The second generation of K-pop idols transformed South Korea's influence worldwide. Their success was massive - K-pop exports jumped from $22 million in 2003 to over $235 million by 2011, making Korean culture a global phenomenon alongside K-dramas.

This was the era when K-pop truly became a cultural ambassador. By 2012, K-pop's influence had grown strong enough throughout Asia to impact **travel patterns**, drawing international fans who saw South Korea as a destination for music and cultural exploration. Idols from groups like Girls' Generation, Super Junior, and BIGBANG became **style icons**, setting trends in fashion and beauty that spread across Asia, while also creating demand in the luxury market through endorsements.

In terms of beauty, **the "K-pop look"** set new standards across Asia, increasing demand for Korean cosmetics and even cosmetic procedures as fans aimed to emulate the features of their favorite stars. K-pop also became a gateway to the Korean **language and culture**; language proficiency test applications rose by 62% from 2009 to 2011 as K-pop lyrics inspired fans to learn Korean.

However, rapid growth brought challenges. Between 2003 and 2012, the debut of over 200 K-pop groups intensified competition, leading to more physically demanding schedules and legal disputes. High-profile cases like TVXQ's 2009 lawsuit against SM Entertainment drew attention to restrictive contracts. These cases highlighted the need for fairer agreements, prompting some reforms by the Korea Fair Trade Commission (KFTC).

The darker side of fame also surfaced through the actions of "*sasaeng*" fans—overzealous followers whose obsession often crossed into harassment. Incidents of stalking and privacy invasion highlighted the need for better protection for idols.

DESPITE THESE CHALLENGES, the second generation laid a solid launch pad for K-pop's future. It was a period of rapid cultural exchange that transformed K-pop from a local trend into a global cultural movement, setting the stage for the industry's next step.

CHAPTER 6
THE CRAFTING OF K-POP
FROM STUDIO TO STAGE

CREATING a K-pop idol or group is a complex process that goes far beyond just making music. It's a process that combines talent, technology, strategy, and artistry into one complete entertainment package.

This chapter breaks down how K-pop agencies craft their perfect products, from the first musical note to the moment a group hits the stage. We'll see how every detail of a K-pop idol's presentation is carefully planned to create not just musicians, but global superstars.

THE MUSIC: MAKING THE PERFECT K-POP HIT

A K-pop release isn't just a collection of songs - it's a complete experience that brings together music, visuals, and storytelling.

In the K-pop industry, entertainment companies typically orchestrate the entire music production process, employing teams of in-house composers, choreographers, and producers to create a perfect product.

Before anything else, teams spend months developing the "concept" - the overall theme and vision of the "comeback" (K-pop term for "new release"). This involves creative directors, stylists, choreographers, visual artists, and marketers all working together. Some examples include:

- BTS's Bangtan Universe (creating an entire fictional world)
- Red Velvet's "Red" and "Velvet" concepts (showing two different sides of the group)

- SEVENTEEN's *An Ode* album (exploring themes of youth)

Sometimes, the song comes first and inspires the concept; other times, it's the other way around. **Korean and international songwriters collaborate**, though the extent of international participation can vary by company and comeback. They draw inspiration from trends, experiences, and even fan feedback. Their goal is to create something catchy but distinctly K-pop.

While much of the music is created by in-house teams, companies sometimes purchase rights to existing songs from international songwriters. These tracks are then adapted to fit the K-pop market, often undergoing significant changes in arrangement and lyrics to align with the group's image and the broader concept.

Once the song is written, it's time to hit the recording booth. Vocalists spend hours perfecting each line, usually recording multiple takes to get that perfect sound. Larger agencies may have dedicated vocal coaches on-site to refine intonation, pronunciation — especially for international releases, and the emotional delivery expected in K-pop. Meanwhile, instrumentalists and programmers work to create the rich, layered soundscapes that characterize many K-pop tracks.

But the magic doesn't stop there. The **mixing and mastering** process is where the song really comes to life. Engineers carefully balance all parts of the song to sound great everywhere, from concert venues to your earbuds. They might even create different versions for streaming platforms versus music shows. This attention to detail helps turn good songs into hits.

While the centralized, in-house production model is most common, there has been a growing number of exceptions where idols actively participate in writing and producing their own music. Artists like BTS, Stray Kids, SEVENTEEN, IU, and G-Dragon are known to contribute significantly to the creative process, offering a more personal touch to their work.

The Talents Outside the Recording Booth

Every K-pop song you love has a talented team working behind the scenes. These producers and composers are the masterminds creating the music that takes over your playlists, and three songwriters/producers stand out in particular.

First, there's **Yoo Young-jin**, SM Entertainment's secret weapon. Known for blending R&B, hip-hop, and electronic sounds, he's helped create SM's signature style, especially in K-pop's early days. If you've ever caught yourself humming H.O.T.'s "Candy" or TVXQ's "Mirotic," you're experiencing Yoo's magic at work.

Over at YG Entertainment, Korean-American rapper **Teddy Park** has been the genius behind some of K-pop's biggest hits. His work with BLACKPINK, BIGBANG, and 2NE1 shows his talent for creating bold, powerful songs that dominate the charts. When you hear a YG track, chances are Teddy's behind it.

Then there's **J.Y. Park**, the founder of JYP Entertainment. More than just a company leader, he's deeply involved in creating music and training artists. His focus on authentic performances has created the distinct "JYP style" you hear in groups like Wonder Girls and TWICE.

What makes K-pop so special is how it blends **different music styles into something new** and exciting. A single song might mix pop, hip-hop, R&B, and rock all at once. Take EXO's "Growl," for example. This track perfectly combines R&B and pop with a swing beat, helping establish EXO's unique sound and becoming a hit across Asia.

Or consider 2NE1's "I Am The Best," produced by Teddy Park. It's pure 2NE1 energy - electronic pop and hip-hop mixed with rock attitude. The powerful beats and confident lyrics perfectly capture 2NE1's fierce image, showing how K-pop producers do more than just make catchy tunes - they create a group's entire musical identity.

These producers don't just write songs; they craft complete experiences that capture hearts worldwide. Each track is carefully designed to match its group's image and connect with fans, making K-pop the global phenomenon it is today.

Fun Fact: *The "JYP whisper" is a softly whispered "J-Y-P" used as a distinctive audio tag in many songs produced by JYP Entertainment. Introduced by founder J.Y. Park, this branding element has become an iconic feature in K-pop, symbolizing his hands-on involvement in production.*

THE DANCE: WHERE K-POP COMES TO LIFE

When you think of K-pop, you probably picture idols moving in perfect sync, their bodies telling a story as compelling as the lyrics they're singing. This is the epitome of K-pop performance – where **music becomes visual art**, and dance becomes a language understood by millions worldwide.

In K-pop, choreography is not just an afterthought stuck onto a music performance; it's an integral, indispensable part of the music. Each move is crafted to complement the song, amplifying its emotional impact and creating a complete audio-visual experience.

Creating these iconic dance routines is an intricate process. Choreographers work with music producers, creative directors, and sometimes the idols themselves to turn the song's message and mood into movement. Take BTS's "Blood Sweat & Tears" as an example. Every move in this dance tells part of a story about struggle and ambition. Fans quickly noticed the "wings" move, where the members spread their arms like wings - it became a signature moment that perfectly captured the song's themes of temptation and desire.

A key element of this process is **"point choreography"** - signature moves designed to be easily recognizable and memorable. These key points often align with the chorus or hook of the song, creating viral moments that fans can instantly identify and replicate. Think of BLACKPINK's finger gun move in "DDU-DU DDU-DU" or TWICE's "TT" hand gesture - these aren't just random movements; they're carefully crafted focal points that help songs become cultural phenomena.

Whether it's joining in at a concert with thousands of others or participating in the latest dance challenge on social media, K-pop choreography transforms passive listeners into **active participants** in a global community.

But getting these performances to look effortless takes serious work. K-pop idols often practice for 10-12 hours a day during busy periods. All this dedication is what creates those jaw-dropping moments when groups like EXO or TWICE move so perfectly together that they look like one person multiplied across the stage.

That's what makes K-pop dance so special. Behind every viral move are months of hard work from both the artists and their choreographers, all working to create something that will stick in your head just as much as the song itself. It doesn't matter if you don't speak Korean - when you see these dances, you just get it. That's the magic of K-pop - it brings people together through dance, no translation needed.

The Talents Behind the Moves

Behind these incredible performances are some of the most talented choreographers in the industry. **Lia Kim**, for instance, has been the creative force behind iconic routines for groups like TWICE, with hits like "TT" showcasing her ability to craft cute, catchy moves that fans around the world can easily follow. As co-founder of 1MILLION Dance Studio, she works with a team of choreographers who contribute to many well-loved K-pop routines.

Entertainment companies invest heavily in choreography, hiring and flying in notable choreographers from wherever they are around the world. A good example is **Keone Madrid**, an American choreographer who has made a big mark in the K-pop world. His work with BTS on songs like "Dope" and "Fire" brought fresh, street-dance influences to K-pop, known for its intricate footwork and dynamic formations that push the boundaries of what K-pop dance can be.

Other renowned international choreographers behind those iconic K-pop dances include **Parris Goebel**, **Kyle Hanagami**, and **Rina Nakasone**.

MUSIC VIDEO PRODUCTION: VISUAL STORYTELLING

K-pop music videos are masterclasses in visual storytelling - they're cinematic experiences that fans anticipate just as eagerly as the songs themselves. Whether narrative-driven or focused purely on performance, **high-quality production** is a defining characteristic of K-pop music videos. Major companies spend a lot of money on these productions; but even groups with more modest budgets have to live up to the high standards that have become expected with K-pop.

Creating a K-pop music video is essentially producing a short film, involving teams of directors, cinematographers, set designers, visual effects artists, lighting technicians, and costume designers, among others. Some videos feature elaborate sets, multiple locations, and complex storylines. For instance, BTS's "Spring Day" music video is so rich in symbolism that you have to watch it several times to fully appreciate it.

The technical execution is just as sophisticated. Strategic cinematography, dynamic editing, and precisely timed transitions create a visually engaging experience that enhances the impact of each performance. This is particularly evident in dance-focused videos, where camera work is choreographed as carefully as the movements it captures.

THE LOOK: CRAFTING THE IMAGE

Looking good is just as important as sounding good in K-pop. The carefully crafted image of each idol and group translates directly to their overall appeal and success.

These artists aren't just picking random clothes from their closets. Agencies hire teams of stylists, costume designers, hairstylists, and makeup artists to have the idols look their best and in line with the concept of each comeback. From the colorful, coordinated outfits of TWICE to the chic, high-fashion ensembles of BLACKPINK, each group's style becomes an integral part of their identity.

Signature hair colors and styles often become iconic looks, adding to each idol's uniqueness. Think of G-Dragon's ever-changing hair colors, which helped cement his trendsetter status, or TWICE's Dahyun's platinum blonde, which fans couldn't stop talking about. In K-pop, makeup goes beyond enhancing natural features; it's an art form that can transform idols' appearances to match various concepts, from fresh and natural to bold and *avant-garde*.

While the focus is primarily on styling, it can't be denied that some companies might also suggest cosmetic procedures to keep up with beauty trends and standards.

Brand Partnerships and Endorsements

K-pop stars aren't just entertainers - they're powerful cultural influencers. Major brands know that when a K-pop idol promotes something, fans pay attention; they are highly sought-after **brand ambassadors**, representing everything from cosmetics to technology. These partnerships are carefully chosen to match each star's image and appeal to their fan base.

Take BTS's collaboration with Samsung, for example. The tech company knew that having BTS film music videos on their phones would make their products instantly cooler to young people worldwide, but it also gave BTS a global platform to showcase their artistry with smartphone-filmed music videos.

The beauty industry especially loves K-pop stars. Groups like BLACK-PINK have become faces of **major beauty brands**, with members often releasing their own makeup collections. When Lisa partnered with MAC Cosmetics, she didn't just slap her name on the products - she helped design a collection that reflected her personal style, giving fans a chance to connect with her through makeup.

Fashion is another important area in K-pop territory. Idols often serve as ambassadors for luxury fashion houses, bridging the gap between high fashion and pop culture. G-Dragon's partnership with Chanel, for instance, helped transform the classic fashion house's image, making it appeal to a whole new generation across Asia and beyond.

These partnerships do double duty - they're not just about making money; they help establish K-pop stars as major cultural influencers who shape trends well beyond the music industry.

The "Perfect" Image: Managing Idol Life for Perfection

In the world of K-pop, an idol's image is as meticulously choreographed as their dance routines. Entertainment agencies exercise great control over their stars' public personas, carefully maintaining a pristine and marketable image; they manage **every aspect of their idols' lives** — beyond public appearances and performances, extending influence over their personal lives and public behavior.

This especially holds true during the idols' trainee years and early in their careers, when agencies are still trying to establish their artists' professional image as role models embodying virtues of hard work, respect, and dedication.

Agencies may set strict guidelines for idols' diets, exercise routines, and living arrangements, and even occasionally manage their education. Many rookie idols live in company dormitories, with their days structured around intensive training and performance schedules.

Social media presence requires particular attention in today's digital age. While established artists may enjoy more freedom, most idol accounts are monitored by agency staff to maintain consistency with their public image. Even personal messages to fans often go through a review process to ensure they align with the group's brand.

Perhaps the most remarkable aspect of this image management is the infamous **"no dating" rule**. Some agencies actually include "no dating" clauses in idol contracts. It is considered best to keep idols "single" and unattached, helping to give their young fans an illusion of attainability — or at least, availability.

Some companies keep this dating ban in place for years, usually loosening up once their stars get older or super successful. But when K-pop stars do date, the fan reaction can be intense. When Bae Suzy of Miss A was found to be dating actor Lee Min-ho in 2015, it was huge news, but had little negative impact on her career because she already had a strong fanbase. But lesser-known idols often get punished more harshly, putting their careers and agencies at great risk.

Though this level of control is often justified as necessary in the competitive K-pop industry, it has sparked discussions about ethics and sustainability, particularly regarding idols' mental health and personal freedom. Balancing a marketable image with personal authenticity remains an ongoing challenge in the industry.

When Things Go Wrong: Damage Control in K-pop

If something does happen and controversy arises, as it always does — e.g., an idol is caught dating someone or gets accused of having bullied someone in middle school — agencies are ready with their playbook. They have developed sophisticated strategies to manage inconvenient situations.

One common tactic is the use of **"hiatuses"**—temporary "timeouts" from public activities that buy time while waiting for negative publicity to die down. Agencies often present these hiatuses as giving the idols "time for self-reflection" — an approach that aligns well with East Asian values of humility and introspection while aiming to restore public goodwill.

In more serious cases, companies might choose to **remove someone** from the group to protect everyone else's reputation. An example of this would be Seungri from BIGBANG. When he got into legal trouble, YG Entertainment decided it was better to remove him than risk damaging the whole group's or the agency's image.

Companies often have their idols get involved in **charity work or public service** to counterbalance negative press. This can help repair an idol's public image by showing them as caring and socially responsible. But it's not a reliable approach, as fans may or may not buy it.

THE ROLES: CRAFTING GROUP DYNAMICS

A K-pop group is a carefully assembled team, where each member plays a specific part in the group's success. While more groups are beginning to break traditional molds, most still follow these established roles:

- **Leader**: Usually the oldest or most experienced member who guides the group, handles media interactions, and maintains group harmony. They're the group's spokesperson and mediator.
- **Main Vocalist**: The most skilled singer who handles the most challenging vocal parts and showcases the group's musical talent.
- **Main Dancer**: The most skilled dancer; they often help other members with dance practice.
- **Main Rapper**: The most skilled rapper who delivers and helps shape the group's musical style.
- **Lead Vocalist(s)**: Members who are highly skilled singers but considered just below the "main" level; multiple members can be "Lead"s.
- **Lead Dancer(s)**: Members who are highly skilled dancers but considered just below the "main" level; multiple members can be "Lead"s.
- **Lead Rapper(s)**: Members who are highly skilled rappers but considered just below the "main" level; multiple members can be "Lead"s.
- **Center**: The member placed at the forefront during performances and promotions, chosen for their charisma, visuals, and stage presence. This role may rotate or be assigned permanently.
- **Visual:** The member considered most attractive in terms of physical appearance. They often become the group's face in advertisements and media.
- **Maknae**: The youngest member, often portrayed as cute or playful to appeal to fans, bringing energy and freshness to the group's dynamic.
- **All-Rounder**: Versatile members who can fill multiple roles effectively, providing stability and flexibility to the group's performances.

These assigned roles create a balanced group dynamic and give each member a distinct identity, allowing fans to choose favorites while supporting the group as a whole.

Subunits: Breaking Down K-pop Groups into Smaller Teams

K-pop companies often create smaller teams within their main groups - called "subunits" - to showcase different talents and styles.

Subunits serve several strategic purposes:

- **Spotlight Individual Talents:** Some members might have amazing skills that don't get enough attention in the full group. Subunits let these talents shine - one subunit might focus on the strongest vocalists while another on the best dancers.
- **Explore Different Styles:** While the main group might be known for bright, energetic pop, a subunit could experiment with R&B or hip-hop without changing the group's core identity.
- **Keep Fans Engaged:** When the full group is in between releases or otherwise inactive, companies keep fans engaged by having subunits release music or content. This steady stream of content keeps the fans excited and maintains buzz and media attention.
- **Get Into Regional Markets**: By featuring members who are from or popular in certain areas or countries, or by adapting music styles and themes to regional tastes, companies can use subunits to widen their market reach.
- **Test Market Potential:** Before trying something new with the whole group, companies can test different concepts or spotlight certain members through subunits to see how fans react.
- **Manage Busy Schedules:** With some groups having 10+ members, subunits make it easier to manage schedules. While some members are busy with acting or other projects, others can promote in smaller teams.

Notable examples of successful subunits include:

- **Super Junior-K.R.Y**: A vocal-focused subunit highlighting the main vocalists of Super Junior.
- **EXO-CBX:** Known for a musical style distinct from EXO's usual sound, appealing to a broader audience.
- **EXO's Market-Specific Subunits**:
  - **EXO-K**: Focused on Korean promotions.
  - **EXO-M**: Targeted the Chinese-speaking market, performing songs in Mandarin.
- **NCT's Subunits for Regional Focus**:
  - **WayV**: A Chinese market-focused subunit of NCT with Mandarin-speaking members.

- NCT 127: Based in Seoul, with a strong presence in Japan through regular Japanese releases and the inclusion of Japanese member Yuta.
- **Stray Kids' 3RACHA**: Composed of members Bang Chan, Changbin, and Han, known for composing and producing most of Stray Kids' songs and showcasing their rap and lyrical talents.

K-POP MARKETING: THE JOURNEY FROM START TO STARDOM

Entertainment companies use various, meticulously planned marketing strategies to transform promising trainees into global icons. This process begins in the pre-debut period and generally follows the following pattern:

Building Pre-debut Buzz

Creating anticipation has become an art form in K-pop. Companies engage fans through carefully timed social media campaigns, releasing just enough to captivate interest without revealing too much. BTS's debut is a prime example: despite limited resources, Big Hit Entertainment (now HYBE) introduced each member gradually, building curiosity and enabling fans to connect with individual personalities before the official debut.

The Grand Entrance

Groups typically debut in one of two ways:

1. **Showcase events** where fans and media experience the group through live performances and Q&A sessions.
2. **Television debuts** on high-profile music shows. For instance, BLACKPINK debuted on *Inkigayo*, marking a confident entry backed by YG Entertainment.

Weekly Music Show Circuit

After debuting, groups participate in the competitive weekly music show circuit, performing on programs like *M Countdown*, *Music Bank*, and *Inkigayo*. These appearances involve unique choreography, special outfits, and creative staging, in order to compete for first-place trophies. The atmosphere is enhanced by synchronized fan chants, creating an immersive experience that strengthens the bond between artists and audiences.

Digital Fan Engagement

Social media has revolutionized how K-pop groups connect with fans. Beyond traditional platforms like Twitter and Instagram, specialized apps like Weverse and V Live enable direct interaction between idols and their supporters. This constant connection maintains fan engagement and creates a sense of intimacy despite physical distances.

Global Expansion

With rising popularity, many K-pop groups expand globally, organizing **world tours** and hosting events. Pre-COVID, **fan meetings** and **hi-touch events** offered cherished face-to-face moments. Some campaigns, like BTS's *Love Yourself* series, transcended entertainment by combining musical impact with messages of self-acceptance. Through a partnership with UNICEF, this campaign promoted mental health awareness and anti-violence, amplifying BTS's influence on a global scale.

We will cover K-pop's global expansion strategies in more detail later in Chapter 10.

Fun Fact: RM, BTS's leader, personally wrote much of the heartfelt English speech he delivered at the UN in 2018. His powerful message of self-acceptance and empowerment resonated globally, marking BTS as the first K-pop group to address the UN.

PRODUCT PACKAGING AND MERCHANDISING

K-pop album packaging is an art form, often designed and crafted as elaborate, collectible items:

- **Extras Inside**: Physical albums frequently include photo cards, posters, and mini-books, turning them into coveted collectibles.
- **Multiple Versions**: Albums may be released in multiple versions with unique designs to offer fans variety and encourage multiple purchases. For example, EXO's *Don't Mess Up My Tempo* album came in different versions, each celebrating a distinct era of rock music through its design.
- **Limited Editions**: Some albums come in limited editions with premium materials or special visual effects, enhancing their appeal.

These approaches make albums valuable to fans as collectibles that they "just gotta have," creating an immersive experience that goes beyond the music itself.

Merchandising

K-pop merchandise extends beyond typical music items to include:

- **Customized Light Sticks**: Every major group has its own signature light stick - a unique device that fans wave at concerts, creating mesmerizing patterns of centrally-controlled, synchronized lights. These aren't just regular glow sticks - they're carefully designed symbols of fan identity.
- **Character Merch**: Some groups create plush toys or merchandise based on mascots or avatars. BTS collaborated with LINE FRIENDS to create BT21, a collection of adorable characters designed by the members themselves. These characters appear on everything from plush toys to school supplies, letting fans have a piece of BTS at home.
- **Lifestyle Products**: From clothing to accessories, K-pop groups release lifestyle products featuring logos or designs inspired by the members, allowing fans to incorporate their favorite groups into daily life.

Through these well-designed products, K-pop groups create tangible connections with their fans, turning music appreciation into a more personal, interactive experience.

CRAFTING the perfect K-pop package is an art form that continues to evolve. From the meticulous process of music production to the innovative use of technology for fan engagement, every aspect is carefully considered and refined. K-pop's global success is a testament to the industry's ability to create a complete entertainment experience that goes beyond music—combining stunning performances, engaging personalities, and a deep connection with fans.

CHAPTER 7

THE TITANS OF K-POP
THE THIRD GENERATION'S GLOBAL BREAKTHROUGH: 2012-2017

AS 2012 BEGAN, K-pop was about to enter an exciting new chapter. Over the next five years, a fresh wave of K-pop groups would emerge - known as the third generation - and they would change the global music scene forever. These artists didn't just top the charts in Korea; they helped turn K-pop from a local success story into something the whole world would eagerly embrace.

ANOTHER PERFECT STORM: THE ECONOMY, TECHNOLOGY, AND HALLYU 2.0

What made this global success possible? It was perfect timing. South Korea's **economy** recovered and rebounded well from the 2008 global financial crisis. Between 2010 and 2017, the country's economy grew impressively from $1.09 trillion to $1.53 trillion, giving entertainment companies the resources they needed to think bigger.

At the same time, **technology** was bringing people closer together than ever before. In South Korea, smartphones went from being somewhat rare to being everywhere - only about 22% of people had them in 2011, but by 2017, nearly everyone did (87%). The same thing was happening globally, with smartphone users jumping from 1 billion to 3 billion people, opening up a vast audience for K-pop.

Music streaming services also changed how people discovered new music. While **Spotify** (launched in 2008) wasn't available in South Korea until 2021, globally, it grew from 15 million users in 2012 to 170 million by 2017. This meant that a teenager in Brazil or Canada could easily stumble upon and fall in love with a K-pop song.

YouTube became especially instrumental in spreading K-pop around the world. By 2012, K-pop videos were getting billions of views each year. When PSY's "Gangnam Style" became the first YouTube video ever to reach a billion views in December 2012, it was a watershed moment for K-pop's global visibility.

Recognizing the power of its cultural exports, the South Korean government further increased its support. Under the "**Hallyu 2.0**" program, they more than doubled their funding for cultural promotion — from $182 million in 2009 to over $420 million by 2017.

The stage was set for K-pop's next chapter. Groups that debuted during this era would transform from local stars into global icons, achieving levels of international success that the earlier generations could only dream of.

DEFINING FEATURES AND INDUSTRY INNOVATIONS

When the third generation of K-pop stars burst onto the scene between 2012 and 2017, they had something special going for them: an entertainment industry that was dreaming bigger than ever. While these groups carried forward the best of what earlier stars had built, they also had the advantage of companies that were getting savvier about reaching global audiences. This powerful combination of talented artists and an evolving industry would help K-pop conquer new territory worldwide:

Masters of Social Media: K-pop stars became incredibly savvy at connecting with fans online, making **Twitter** and **Instagram** their virtual homes away from home. Take BTS, for instance - by 2017, they had built up a massive Twitter following that would make most celebrities jealous. These platforms let artists chat directly with fans and share snippets of their daily lives, whether through funny selfies or behind-the-scenes moments. Even when artists and fans didn't speak the same language, a heart emoji or a liked post could speak volumes, helping build devoted fan communities all around the world.

Training for a Global Stage: K-pop's famously intense training system got even more ambitious. Entertainment companies knew that to truly go global, their artists needed more than just perfect dance moves and flawless vocals. They started putting serious emphasis on **language**

learning, getting their artists ready to communicate in English, Japanese, and even Spanish. This meant idols could connect with fans around the world in their own languages, making interviews and meet-and-greets more personal. **Cultural training** also became part of the curriculum, with companies preparing idols not only to perform but also to navigate diverse cultural settings, preparing their stars to be cultural ambassadors who could confidently represent K-pop and South Korea wherever they went.

Going Global from Day One: The K-pop industry started getting bolder with its launch strategies, with some groups setting their sights on international success from day one. GOT7's 2014 debut was a perfect example - they hit the ground running with showcases in both South Korea and Japan. While most groups still focused on making it big at home first, this new approach showed how the industry was changing its mindset. Instead of conquering Korea before looking abroad, some companies were ready to take their artists global from the very beginning.

Taking Music Videos and Albums to the Next Level: K-pop videos started looking more like mini-movies, with stunning visuals and rich storytelling. BTS really raised the bar in 2015 with "I Need U," which kicked off their epic "BTS Universe" storyline - suddenly, fans weren't just watching music videos; they were hunting for hidden meanings and connections. Albums became artistic experiences, too. When EXO dropped *EXODUS* in 2015, they gave each member their own special album cover. Groups started weaving entire stories and themes through their albums. It wasn't just about the songs anymore - fans were getting pulled into whole artistic worlds that they could explore and theorize about.

Mix and Match Promotions: Entertainment companies got clever about keeping fans excited all year long by letting group members branch out between main comebacks. Some artists would team up to form subunits, while others got to shine solo. BTS's Suga transformed into Agust D in 2016, showing fans a whole different side of himself. Groups like Red Velvet played with this formula, too, switching things up with different combinations of members. It was a win-win: fans got fresh content to enjoy, and artists got to experiment with new styles and sounds.

K-Drama and K-pop Synergies: K-pop and K-drama grew stronger together, each industry amplifying the other's success. Popular idols found new creative outlets through acting roles, while their music became an integral part of drama soundtracks. This crossover approach proved highly effective - fans could enjoy their favorite performers in multiple contexts, while Korean entertainment as a whole gained a stronger global foothold. Together, these industries helped establish Korea as a major force in modern entertainment.

International Collaborations: Collaborations with Western artists used to be rare, but as K-pop grew bigger, they became increasingly common. BTS recorded songs with Halsey and Steve Aoki, while BLACKPINK joined forces with Dua Lipa. These partnerships did more than just create great music - they helped K-pop reach new fans worldwide and showed that pop music didn't need to be in English to be huge. It changed the whole game of what it means to be an international superstar.

Genre Experimentation: Pushing musical boundaries, third-generation groups experimented with a large variety of genres. BTS expanded their repertoire from hip-hop into pop, rock, EDM, and beyond, while TWICE transitioned from "cute" concepts to more mature themes. This willingness to experiment with different music styles helped third-gen groups attract all kinds of music fans, from rock lovers to pop enthusiasts.

Fandom Ecosystem: The connection between K-pop stars and their fans grew stronger than ever during this time. Official fan clubs and online communities like EXO's EXO-L (established in 2014) offered fans exclusive content and a closer connection to their idols. While today's platforms like **Lysn** and **Weverse** weren't around yet, the third generation set the stage for today's vibrant fandom ecosystems, giving fans dedicated spaces to come together and support their favorite groups.

Global Concert Tours: K-pop concerts became truly international events during this time. When BTS launched *The Wings* tour in 2017, they performed across 17 cities in Asia, North and South America, and Oceania. These **massive international tours** showed just how popular K-pop had become and helped create an even bigger worldwide following. Fans who once could only watch their favorite groups online could now experience the excitement of live performances in their own countries.

K-pop Stars as Cultural Ambassadors: K-pop artists became representatives of South Korean culture worldwide. A defining moment came during the 2018 Winter Olympics in Pyeongchang, when the group EXO performed at the closing ceremony. Millions of people around the world watched them perform at this prestigious international event. K-pop stars were now unofficial cultural ambassadors of Korea.

The third generation of K-pop artists emerged at just the right time. Having grown up in a connected world, they understood how to reach international audiences and use technology to their advantage. Their determination and skills helped K-pop become more popular than ever before. These artists' success opened doors for newer K-pop stars to connect with fans globally.

NOTABLE THIRD-GENERATION K-POP IDOLS AND THEIR IMPACTS

EXO (2012-Present, SM Ent.): Debuted with an innovative dual-subunit concept (EXO-K for Korea, EXO-M for China). Their debut showcase at Seoul's Olympic Stadium showed SM's confidence in the group. *MAMA* (2012) introduced their supernatural powers concept, setting a new standard for K-pop storytelling. Their album *XOXO* (2013) became the first million-seller in Korea in 12 years since g.o.d's *Chapter 4*.

BTOB (2012-Present, Cube Ent.): Known for exceptional vocal abilities, BTOB balanced a playful "beagle-dol" image with serious musicianship. Their shift to ballads with *It's Okay* (2015) showcased their versatility, and Sungjae's role in *Goblin* (2016), a popular TV drama, boosted the group's popularity.

VIXX (2012–2023, Jellyfish Ent.): Dubbed the "concept kings" of K-pop, VIXX redefined idol group storytelling with dark, theatrical themes in hits like "Voodoo Doll" (2013) and "Shangri-La" (2017). Their innovative use of visuals and narrative-driven performances influenced the industry, making them a standout group of the third generation.

BTS (2013-Present, Big Hit/now HYBE): The undisputed kings of K-pop that revolutionized K-pop's global reach. Their album *Wings* (2016) became the first K-pop album to chart for multiple weeks on *Billboard 200*, and "DNA" (2017) was the first K-pop group MV to hit 1 billion views on YouTube. Their 2018 speech at the UN for UNICEF's *Generation Unlimited* campaign launch elevated K-pop's cultural impact, with their *Love Myself* campaign promoting mental health and self-love. Their fandom, ARMY, has set new standards for organized fan activities and philanthropy.

Sunmi (solo, 2013-Present, JYP Ent.): Her "24 Hours" (2013) marked a successful transition from Wonder Girls to soloist, and "Gashina" (2017) went viral for its choreography, solidifying her status as a top solo artist.

CL (solo, 2013-Present, YG Ent.): As the former leader of 2NE1, CL's solo career embodied K-pop's expanding global ambitions. Her debut single, "The Baddest Female" (2013), showcased her fierce rap style. She then gained visibility in the U.S. market with her collaboration on "Doctor Pepper" (2015) with Diplo. Finally, her English single "Lifted" (2016) broke new ground, making her the first female K-pop soloist to chart on the *Billboard Hot 100* and further solidifying her presence in the Western music scene.

RED VELVET (2014-Present, SM Ent.): Known for their dual "red" (vibrant) and "velvet" (smooth) concepts, "Russian Roulette" (2016) showcased their quirky style. They were among the first K-pop acts to perform in North Korea in 2018.

GOT7 (2014-Present, JYP Ent.): A multinational group known for acrobatic performances, GOT7's "Just Right" (2015) gained attention for its positive message. Jackson's solo work expanded their reach in China, and their departure from JYP in 2021 while retaining the group name set a precedent in K-pop.

Fun Fact: GOT7 made history as one of the first K-pop groups to hold a fan meeting in the Middle East. In 2017, they hosted a fan event in Dubai, United Arab Emirates.

MAMAMOO (2014-Present, RBW Ent.): Renowned for powerful vocals and live performances, "Um Oh Ah Yeh" (2015) displayed their retro and humorous style. Solar's appearance on *We Got Married* (2016) further increased their variety show presence.

WINNER (2014-Present, YG Ent.): Known for self-composing and producing, WINNER gained massive popularity with "Empty" (2014) right after debuting. Their versatile style and strong public presence helped solidify YG's place among the third generation.

Akdong Musician (AKMU) (2014-Present, YG Ent.): The brother and sister duo AKMU brought a fresh, unique sound to K-pop. Known for their meaningful lyrics and acoustic style, their album *Play* (2014) had major chart success.

TWICE (2015-Present, JYP Ent.): TWICE initially dominated with their "cute" concept before evolving into a more mature style. "Cheer Up"

(2016) popularized the phrase "shy shy shy," and their Japanese debut set records for K-pop girl groups in Japan. Tzuyu was ranked the most beautiful face in the world by TC Candler in 2019.

SEVENTEEN (2015-Present, Pledis Ent.): Known as a self-producing group, SEVENTEEN's "Don't Wanna Cry" (2017) showcased their emotional depth. Their *Going Seventeen* YouTube series set new standards for idol-driven content.

MONSTA X (2015-Present, Starship Ent.): Known for intense performances and a powerful style, "Hero" (2015) solidified their image. MONSTA X became the first K-pop group on iHeartRadio's Jingle Ball tour in 2018.

iKON (2015-Present, YG Ent.): iKON's debut single "My Type" (2015) achieved an all-kill on Korean charts, and "Love Scenario" (2018) became a cultural phenomenon, especially popular among young listeners.

GFRIEND (2015-2021, Source Music): Known for "powerful innocence" and precise choreography; "Rough" (2016) set records with 15 music show wins, a milestone for girl groups.

DAY6 (2015-Present, JYP Ent.): Known as a pop-rock band, DAY6's "Congratulations" (2015) showcased emotional storytelling. Their *Every DAY6* project (2017), releasing music monthly, set a new standard for regular comebacks.

Taeyeon (solo, 2015-Present, SM Ent.): This Girls' Generation member's solo debut "I" (2015) topped charts, and "Fine" (2017) reinforced her status as one of K-pop's top soloists.

BLACKPINK (2016-Present, YG Ent.): BLACKPINK skyrocketed to stardom. "Whistle" (2016) won on *Inkigayo* just 14 days after debut, a record for girl groups, and "DDU-DU DDU-DU" (2018) became the most-viewed K-pop group MV. They made history as the first K-pop girl group to perform at Coachella in 2019. Largely seen as the female counterpart to BTS.

NCT (2016-Present, SM Ent.): NCT introduced an innovative "infinite member" concept with multiple subunits. NCT 127's "Fire Truck" (2016) highlighted their experimental style, and NCT DREAM's "Chewing Gum" (2016) featured hoverboard choreography, showcasing SM's technological flair.

ASTRO (2016-Present, Fantagio): Known for a positive and "bright" concept, "Breathless" (2016) emphasized synchronized choreography. Cha Eunwoo's acting in *My ID is Gangnam Beauty* (2018) significantly increased ASTRO's visibility.

PENTAGON (2016-Present, Cube Ent.): Self-producing group known for diverse concepts, PENTAGON's "Shine" (2018) went viral for its catchy choreography and showcased the members' songwriting skills.

SF9 (2016-Present, FNC Ent.): FNC's first dance-focused boy group, SF9 became known for sharp choreography, with "Roar" (2017) exemplifying their style. Rowoon's acting in *Extraordinary You* (2019) brought the group more attention.

The Boyz (2017-Present, IST Entertainment): Known for their high-energy, synchronized performances, The Boyz gained acclaim for their choreography and stage presence. Winning *Road to Kingdom* on Mnet in 2020 solidified their reputation as performance leaders, helping them expand internationally, especially in Japan.

Jackson Wang (solo, 2017-Present, Team Wang): GOT7's Jackson successfully launched a solo career, especially in China, with "Papillon" (2017) marking his debut. He founded his own label, Team Wang, and balances group and solo activities across music, fashion, and media.

Dreamcatcher (2017-Present, Dreamcatcher Company): Stood out with their rock-influenced sound and horror-inspired visuals, debuting with "Chase Me" (2017). Their unique concept and dark storytelling earned them a dedicated global fanbase, proving that alternative styles could thrive in K-pop.

Wanna One (2017-2019, Swing Ent.): A boy group born from *Produce 101 Season 2*, Wanna One became an instant sensation with "Energetic" (2017), achieving chart all-kills and record-breaking sales. Their success as a temporary group redefined the impact of survival show-created acts.

LEGACY OF INFLUENCE AND IMPACT

The third generation of K-pop marked a new phase in the genre's expansion — they went **from regional to global**. Between 2012 and 2017, K-pop exports more than doubled, growing from $235 million to approximately $513 million, showing just how popular it had become internationally.

But the real story wasn't just in the numbers - it was in how these groups changed popular culture around the world. With groups like BTS and BLACKPINK leading the charge, K-pop influenced everything from **tourism**—turning South Korea into a "must-visit" destination for international fans—to **fashion** and beauty. Luxury brands — including major European ones — eagerly sought these idols as ambassadors, while **K-beauty** products gained popularity, helping South Korea's cosmetics exports reach nearly $5 billion by 2017.

Beyond fashion, K-pop inspired a wave of interest in the Korean **language and culture**. For example, applications for the Korean proficiency test (TOPIK) nearly tripled from 2012 to 2017. Fans were drawn not only to the music but to the culture that third-generation idols embodied.

Fun Fact: *In 1957, South Korea began to require all males aged 18-28 to serve in the military for 18-21 months; no exceptions! — until… In 2020, a special law was passed allowing K-pop stars who contribute significantly to national culture (translation: economy) to defer their enlistment until age 30, inspired by BTS's global success. Jin was the first BTS member to enlist under this law at age 30 in December 2022, followed by J-Hope and Suga in 2023. The younger members—RM, Jimin, V, and Jungkook—began their service in December 2023, ranging in age from 26 to 29, fulfilling their duties while making history as global icons.*

Yet, rapid success brought new challenges. Over 300 groups debuted between 2012 and 2017, further intensifying the competitive pressure on performers. The psychological toll on idols became more visible, with high-profile cases highlighting struggles with mental health. The double-edged sword of social media, while connecting artists with global audiences, also exposed them to privacy invasions and cyberbullying. Questions about cultural sensitivity emerged as K-pop's influence spread across diverse global audiences.

EVEN WITH THESE CHALLENGES, this generation of K-pop stars did something remarkable - they turned Korean pop music into a worldwide movement. They didn't just top music charts; they changed how people around the world think about entertainment, fashion, and culture. By late 2017, it was clear that K-pop had firmly secured its place on the global stage — not only as a genre of music, but as a driving force in shaping global pop culture.

CHAPTER 8

THE K-POP FANDOM
THE HEART OF THE GLOBAL PHENOMENON

AS OUR STORY moves from third to fourth-generation K-pop stars, let's pause for a moment to look at something truly special: the incredible world of K-pop fans. As incredible as the artists are, K-pop would not have become what it is today without the powerful forces of the passionate fan community behind it.

K-pop fandom is something unique in the entertainment world. These aren't just passive music listeners - they are active players in shaping the K-pop industry and its stars' success. So before we continue our journey through K-pop's generations, let's take a closer look at how these dedicated fans became the beating heart of K-pop's success story.

THE BIRTH OF A MOVEMENT

The story of K-pop fandom began in the 1990s, alongside the rise of first-generation idols. As we explored in Chapter 2, H.O.T.'s "Club H.O.T" and Sechs Kies' "Yellow Kies" were pioneering fan clubs that set the gold standard for devotion.

Club H.O.T (later dubbed "White Angels") made concerts magical by turning venues white — wearing white outfits and waving white balloons. They created special chants that got whole crowds singing together, and found creative ways to promote their favorite artists — such as renting a truck to drive around Seoul to promote their group's album. The Yellow Kies were just as dedicated, pooling their money for special projects like putting up birthday billboards and giving to charity in their group's name. These early fan projects started traditions that K-pop fans everywhere follow today.

In these early days, fan clubs were old-school - they met in person, published and distributed printed newsletters, and organized face-to-face meetings with their idols. These meetings were not just about seeing the stars; they brought fans together as friends. This sense of community and support became a core part of K-pop culture that still defines it today.

Fun Fact: The concept of fandom names dates back to the 19th century, when devoted admirers of Jane Austen, the English author, were called "Janeites." Long before K-pop, these fans formed a community of like-minded enthusiasts and wore that identity proudly.

FANDOM IN THE DIGITAL AGE

When the year 2000 came around, the internet started to change how K-pop fans connected with each other. Online forums on platforms like **Daum** and **Naver** became virtual gathering places where fans could connect with one another regardless of geography. Now, anyone with the internet could be part of these fan groups, no matter where they lived.

The numbers alone were impressive. For example, TVXQ's "Cassiopeia" fan cafe on Daum boasted over 800,000 members by the mid-2000s — a number that would have been unthinkable in the era of physical fan clubs. BIGBANG's fans (called "V.I.P") became known for their well-organized events online. Super Junior's fans (known as "E.L.F") created smaller fan clubs in different languages so people worldwide could join in.

These online spaces revolutionized fan interaction. Real-time updates about idol schedules and appearances became available, and high-quality photos and **fancams** were widely shared, feeding fans' growing appetite for content. International fans organized to translate Korean media, breaking down language barriers and making contents more accessible for fans everywhere.

The rise of social media in the late 2000s and early 2010s brought K-pop fandom into a new era. **Twitter** was perfect for quick updates and getting K-pop topics trending. **Facebook** groups gave fans a place to have longer conversations and plan events together. By 2021, K-pop-related tweets had reached over 7.5 billion annually — a testament to the fandom's immense global reach and engagement.

This digital transformation also changed how fans interacted with idols. Platforms like **V Live** enabled idols to broadcast directly to fans, with some streams attracting over a million viewers at the same time. **Weverse** and **Bubble**, developed by entertainment companies, took this connection further, offering subscription-based services for fans to receive messages directly from their idols. The distance between fans and idols had never seemed smaller.

THE POWER OF COLLECTIVE ACTION

Today's K-pop fandom is a force to be reckoned with. They have achieved amazing feats through organized, coordinated efforts. **"Streaming parties"** are commonly held events, where fans around the world play their favorite songs on YouTube and Spotify to boost their idols' rankings on the charts.

These aren't casual listening sessions; they're carefully organized campaign events. Fans create detailed schedules showing who should stream when, making sure the songs are playing around the clock across different time zones. They circulate step-by-step guides explaining the right way to stream so their views actually count. Some fans even raise funds to buy streaming passes or subscriptions for those who can't afford them. This truly shows the strength of the community bond.

The results can be staggering. In 2020, when BTS released "Dynamite," their fandom, ARMY, mobilized on a never-seen-before scale. The music video got 101.1 million views in its first 24 hours, setting a YouTube record. Similarly, BLACKPINK fans got their song "How You Like That" to 100 million views in just 32 hours. These numbers reflect not only fandom size but also the level of dedication and organization that sets K-pop fandom apart.

Social media campaigns are another powerful tool in the fandom arsenal. When TWICE released "More & More" in 2020, so many fans were tweeting about it that it became one of the most talked-about topics worldwide. And when BTS released "Permission to Dance" in 2021, fans generated over 5 million tweets within the first hour. Sometimes, fans use social media to show support during tough times - when GOT7 left

JYP, fans kept #GOT7_FOREVER trending for days to show they were still there for the group.

And then there's voting for **music shows and awards.** The 2020 Mnet Asian Music Awards (MAMA) received over 60 million votes, underscoring the passion and commitment of fans. Some fandoms even develop custom apps and websites to track voting numbers and help everyone work together better.

Creative Expressions of Fandom

K-pop fandom goes beyond streaming and voting; it's a fount of creativity. Take **fan art**, for example. On social media sites like Instagram and **DeviantArt**, talented fans share all kinds of amazing artwork. Some draw beautiful, detailed portraits of their favorite artists, while others create fun pictures imagining their favorite stars in magical or fantasy situations. Some fan artists have gained so much recognition that entertainment companies have actually hired them to help design official merchandise.

Fan fiction allows writers to expand the universe of their favorite idols, crafting stories that range from romantic tales to complex alternate realities. On platforms like **Archive of Our Own (AO3)**, BTS-related stories alone number in the hundreds of thousands. Some of these fan stories have been so popular that the writers turned them into their own original books by changing the character names.

Then, there are **fan meet-ups**, where online friends get to meet each other in person. These can be as simple as a group of fans getting together at a coffee shop, or as big as huge events like **KCON**, which has become a giant K-pop convention held around the world. These gatherings help fans feel like they're part of something special and let them share their excitement with others who understand their passion.

Official fan meetings - where fans actually get to meet their favorite stars - are truly special events. For example, when BTS held their 5th Muster "Magic Shop" event in Busan in June 2019, 45,000 fans came to see them over two days. And when EXO announced their fan meeting called *EXOPLANET #3 - The EXO'rDIUM[dot]* in 2017, the 10,000 tickets sold out in less than five minutes.

THE ECONOMIC FORCE OF FANDOM

The economic impact of K-pop fandom is immense, and **album sales** alone tell part of this story. When BTS released their album *Map of the Soul: 7* in 2020, fans bought more than 4.17 million copies in just nine days, setting a record for K-pop albums. BLACKPINK's *The Album* became the first album by a K-pop girl group to reach one million sales. That's how fans make money talk.

Concert tickets are another way fans show their support with their wallets. BTS's *Love Yourself: Speak Yourself* tour in 2019 grossed $116.6 million with approximately 976,000 attendees across 20 shows. The impact extends far beyond ticket sales. When BTS performed in Seoul in 2019, their concerts drew international fans, contributing an estimated $860 million to South Korea's economy through **tourism, transportation, and accommodation spending**. In Chicago, businesses around Soldier Field reported significant boosts in sales during BTS's concert days.

The influence of K-pop fandom on the economy is so big that it has drawn the attention of governments and economists. The Hyundai Research Institute (a group that studies the economy) estimated that BTS alone contributed about $3.6 billion to South Korea's economy in 2019 — including exports, tourism, and other related activities. The K-pop industry was estimated to be worth about $5.74 billion that same year.

This economic power has led to increased recognition of fandom's importance. Companies now consult fan bases on merchandise design and concert planning to better cater to fan preferences. The South Korean government has also acknowledged the role of fans in cultural diplomacy and tourism promotion, recognizing that K-pop fandom has become an economic force as well as a cultural one.

THE SHADOW SIDE OF FANDOM

While most fan activities are positive, it's important to acknowledge the darker aspects of fandom. One of the biggest concerns is **"*sasaeng* fans"** — these are overly obsessive fans who might stalk idols, hack their private accounts online, or even try to break into their hotel rooms. The psychological toll on idols can be heavy, and many have spoken out about the anxiety and stress caused by constant invasions of privacy.

Another big problem is **"fan wars"** - when different fan groups fight with each other. These conflicts between fan bases can escalate from online arguments to more serious fights. Fans argue about music awards, or they get upset when they think other fans are insulting their favorite group, or they fight about which group is more successful. A notable example occurred in 2008, when fans of TVXQ got so angry at Super Junior's fans that they created a large petition demanding that Super Junior gets removed from a major end-of-year music show.

These negative aspects of fandom not only tarnish the image of K-pop fans but also create a toxic environment that takes away from the music and artistry at the heart of K-pop. Addressing these issues is crucial for fostering a healthier and more supportive fan culture in the future.

Fun (?) Fact: Some sasaengs work as "flight attendant fans," booking the same flights as idols to be near them during travel.

THE FUTURE OF K-POP FANDOM: WHAT'S COMING NEXT

K-pop fandom stands out globally through its unique combination of digital coordination, structured communities, and organized support activities. While other fan groups share some of these practices, K-pop fans take it to another level - from their highly organized streaming and voting campaigns to their coordinated charity projects and special traditions like group-specific light sticks. The result is something truly distinctive: a tightly-knit global community that works together like a well-oiled machine, creating a model of fandom that's become influential worldwide.

Going Forward

As K-pop continues to evolve, so too will its fandom. New technologies are opening up exciting possibilities. Soon, fans might be able to use **virtual reality (VR)** and **augmented reality (AR)** to feel like they're right there with their favorite singers or attend special virtual events from home. Additionally, some companies are exploring **blockchain technology** and **NFTs**, potentially allowing fans to own unique digital assets related to their favorite idols —though some fans worry about how these technologies might harm the environment.

Speaking of the environment, more and more fans are concerned about **sustainability**. Fans are increasingly demanding eco-friendly merchandise and socially responsible projects, urging companies to adopt sustainable practices that could significantly reduce the industry's environmental footprint.

As K-pop becomes popular in more places around the world, we're seeing fans in different countries create their own unique ways of showing support. Each culture brings its own special touch to being a K-pop fan, making the global K-pop community even more interesting and diverse.

Interestingly, the skills developed through fandom activities are gaining professional recognition. Social media management, event organization, and digital marketing skills honed through fan projects are becoming valuable in various industries. Some dedicated fans have even turned this expertise into careers, advising companies on fan engagement strategies and bringing their fan community insights into professional settings.

K-pop fandom is a multifaceted phenomenon that goes far beyond music appreciation. It's a dynamic force that shapes the industry, influences global popular culture, and creates lasting connections between artists and fans. From its humble beginnings in the 1990s to its current status as a formidable industry player, K-pop fandom has continuously evolved, adapting to new technologies and expanding its reach.

As K-POP CONTINUES TO GROW, one thing's for sure - the dedicated fans who pour their creativity and passion into supporting their favorite artists will keep being the reason K-pop is so successful worldwide.

CHAPTER 9

THE DIGITAL DEMIGODS OF K-POP

BORN GLOBAL—THE FOURTH GENERATION: 2018-2022

AROUND 2018, K-pop was at another turning point. New groups started appearing — what fans and industry observers now call the "fourth generation." These newcomers stepped into a very different world from the groups before them - K-pop had already become huge worldwide.

Unlike earlier acts, many of these new groups came equipped with global elements from the very beginning. They debuted with English-language content, multinational member lineups, and social media strategies designed to connect with fans both in Korea and all over the world, right now, from the start.

DEFINING FEATURES AND INDUSTRY INNOVATIONS

The New Digital World of K-pop: When the fourth generation of K-pop stars began appearing, they entered a landscape that had become a digital playground where smartphones, social media, and streaming platforms were crucial to success. By 2018, smartphones connected nearly 3 billion people worldwide, and platforms like **Instagram**, **Twitter**, and **TikTok** had transformed into virtual stages where fans and stars could interact. Music streaming services like Spotify, which had 207 million monthly active users by early 2019, completely changed how people discovered and listened to music. YouTube, too, had become essential for music and videos, blending online and offline fan experiences into one.

In this super-connected world, these new K-pop stars emerged as more than just performers - they became digital all-rounders. They took on roles beyond entertainment, becoming content creators, brand representatives, and communicators. Their comfort with technology and ability to speak multiple languages let them connect with fans around the world in real time.

Born Into the Digital Age: Unlike previous generations, these new K-pop stars are true digital natives who grew up with the internet and social media as constant parts of their lives. Born in the late 1990s and early 2000s, they don't just know how to use digital tools - it's part of who they are and how they express themselves. This generation naturally weaves digital storytelling into their public image, making them seem more authentic and approachable to fans.

This led K-pop training to evolve, preparing stars not just for performing but for thriving in the digital world. Entertainment companies placed more emphasis on language education and cultural sensitivity training for their artists, but also expanded traditional training to include:

- **Production and composition skills**, so they could help create their own music
- **Social media management**, teaching them to handle their own online presence
- **Content creation**, preparing them for success on YouTube and TikTok

This focus on digital skills created a new kind of K-pop stars ready to perform, create, and connect globally from day one.

Starting with a Worldwide Audience: These new K-pop stars launched their careers in an already global industry, thanks to the success of artists like PSY, BTS, and BLACKPINK, who came before them. From the start, they were expected to appeal to international fans - this influenced everything from their debut plans to their music style, and even how groups were formed, more often including members from different countries. Many groups now release songs in multiple languages right from the beginning, showing how K-pop has become truly international.

While it's still rare for groups to debut in different countries at the same time, companies use social media and streaming platforms to reach fans everywhere at once, often launching with international fans in mind.

This **global-first approach** is very different from past generations, where becoming international stars was a gradual process. Instead, today's new K-pop stars are expected to make an impact worldwide immediately, dealing with both the opportunities and challenges of instant global visibility.

This marks a new chapter in K-pop, where being tech-savvy and globally minded isn't just helpful - it's *essential* for success, as these new stars push beyond what came before and help make K-pop a truly worldwide phenomenon.

NOTABLE FOURTH-GENERATION IDOLS AND THEIR IMPACTS

Stray Kids (2018-Present, JYP Ent.): Stray Kids quickly emerged as a leading fourth-generation K-pop group, known for their intense, self-produced music that blends hip-hop, rock, and electronic elements. Their victory on Mnet's *Kingdom: Legendary War* (2021) and *Billboard* achievements with *ODDINARY* and *MAXIDENT* in 2022 marked them as industry powerhouses. Their production/rap unit, 3RACHA, is key to their success, consistently engaging fans with content between comebacks.

Fun Fact: JYP Entertainment allowed Stray Kids' leader Bang Chan to hand-pick his seven (originally eight) fellow members, though the group was officially formed through the survival show Stray Kids.

(G)I-DLE (2018-Present, Cube Ent.): Known for their self-produced music and powerful concepts, (G)I-DLE quickly became a standout girl group. Led by Soyeon, the group gained acclaim for hits like "LATATA" and "TOMBOY." Their music often incorporates cultural elements, reflecting the members' diverse backgrounds — including Chinese, Taiwanese, and Thai members.

ATEEZ (2018-Present, KQ Ent.): With their intense performances and pirate-inspired concept, ATEEZ has carved a unique niche in K-pop. Despite being from a smaller agency, they built a massive international fandom through word-of-mouth and social media, with story-driven series like *TREASURE* and *FEVER* showcasing their musical and narrative depth.

LOONA (2018-Present, Blockberry Creative): LOONA's innovative pre-debut project introduced each member individually, helping build a dedicated international fanbase. Their "LOONAVERSE" storyline is a complex concept that has captivated fans around the world.

WOODZ (Cho Seungyoun) (solo, 2018-Present, Yuehua Ent.): Formerly of UNIQ and X1, WOODZ has established himself as a versatile soloist, writing and producing his own music. His mini-album *EQUAL* (2020) showcases his genre-blending style, making him a favorite among fans who appreciate his musical range.

Hwasa (solo, 2019-Present, RBW Ent./P Nation): MAMAMOO's Hwasa made a powerful solo debut with "Twit" (2019) and "Maria" (2020), gaining popularity with her unique style and stage presence. Known for challenging beauty standards, she has become an influential figure in K-pop. She left RBW and signed with P Nation — the agency PSY founded — in 2023.

EVERGLOW (2019-Present, Yuehua Ent.): With their "girl crush" concept and powerful performances, EVERGLOW has attracted a significant international following. Their song "DUN DUN" went viral on TikTok, boosting their global popularity.

ITZY (2019-Present, JYP Ent.): ITZY burst onto the scene with their record-breaking debut "DALLA DALLA," known for their "girl crush" concept and messages of self-confidence. With hits like "ICY" and "WANNABE," ITZY has redefined female representation in K-pop and secured numerous rookie awards.

TXT (TOMORROW X TOGETHER) (2019-Present, Big Hit Ent.): Often dubbed BTS's "little brothers" due to their shared label, TXT has captivated audiences with a "youth" concept, blending genres to explore coming-of-age themes in albums like *The Dream Chapter* and *The Chaos Chapter*. Known for their strong conceptual approach, TXT quickly won several rookie awards.

ONEUS (2019-Present, RBW Ent.): Known for theatrical performances and diverse concepts, ONEUS has gained attention through their music videos and live stages, showcasing a unique storytelling approach that sets them apart within the fourth generation.

SOMI (solo, 2019-Present, The Black Label): Former I.O.I member Somi made her solo debut with "Birthday." Her song "DUMB DUMB" (2021) highlighted a mature image and achieved commercial success.

Kang Daniel (solo, 2019-Present, Konnect Ent.): As the former center of Wanna One, Kang Daniel transitioned smoothly to a solo career. His debut EP, *Color on Me,* set records for soloist album sales, solidifying his position in the industry.

aespa (2020-Present, SM Ent.): Pioneering a futuristic concept with AI integration, aespa blends real members with virtual avatars. Hits like "Black Mamba" and "Next Level" showcase their unique sound and story-driven approach. Their Coachella performance as rookies underscores their rapid rise in the industry.

ENHYPEN (2020-Present, Belift Lab): Formed through the survival show *I-LAND,* ENHYPEN captivated fans with their dark, narrative-driven concepts like *BORDER* and *DIMENSION.* Known for synchronized choreography and genre-blending, they have achieved significant success on global charts.

P1Harmony (2020-Present, FNC Ent.): Debuting with a feature film, P1Harmony showcases strong rap skills and socially conscious lyrics, gaining attention with songs like "Siren" and "Do It Like This." Their storytelling approach across multiple media platforms sets them apart.

STAYC (2020-Present, High Up Ent.): Known for their retro-inspired sound and catchy tracks, STAYC has quickly become a leading fourth-generation girl group, building a loyal fanbase with hits like "ASAP" and "STEREOTYPE."

TREASURE (2020-Present, YG Ent.): Debuting with "Boy" (2020), TREASURE quickly gained an international fanbase. Known for dynamic choreography and self-produced music, hits like "JIKJIN" (2022) solidified their status as a fourth-generation leader.

CRAVITY (2020-Present, Starship Ent.): CRAVITY debuted with "Break All the Rules" (2020), showcasing sharp performances and consistent chart success. Their diverse sound and rapid growth have made them a standout fourth-gen group.

KINGDOM (2021-Present, GF Ent.): KINGDOM's unique historical and fantasy-inspired concepts, starting with "Excalibur" (2021), set them apart. Each member represents a different king, blending storytelling and music to captivate fans.

IVE (2021-Present, Starship Ent.): IVE made an immediate impact with "ELEVEN," achieving high rankings on Korean music charts. Known for their sophisticated image and polished performances, they quickly rose to prominence within the fourth-generation scene.

PURPLE KISS (2021-Present, RBW Ent.): Showcasing strong vocals and self-produced music, PURPLE KISS has become a group to watch. Some members contribute to writing and composing, adding to their unique identity in K-pop.

Xdinary Heroes (2021-Present, JYP Ent.): Bringing a rock-band style to JYP's lineup, Xdinary Heroes stands out with a fresh, rock-inspired sound. Their debut song, "Happy Death Day," marked them as a unique addition to the fourth generation, resonating with fans of instrument-based performances.

TRI.BE (2021-Present, TR Ent. & Universal Music Group): With a multi-cultural lineup and genre-blending style, TRI.BE incorporates Afrobeat, Latin, and hip-hop influences. Songs like "DOOM DOOM TA" highlight their experimental sound and international appeal.

LE SSERAFIM (2022–Present, Source Music): Debuting with "FEARLESS", quickly gained attention for their confident themes, polished performances, and experimental style. Hits like "ANTIFRAGILE" have established them as a standout fourth-generation girl group.

Fun Fact: LE SSERAFIM's name is an anagram of "I'm Fearless."

NewJeans (2022-Present, ADOR): With a retro-modern concept blending 90s and Y2K aesthetics, NewJeans quickly gained acclaim with hits like "Attention" and "Hype Boy." Their unique style and innovative debut strategy have set new trends in K-pop.

NMIXX (2022-Present, JYP Ent.): Known for their "mixx pop" genre, NMIXX debuted with "O.O," which showcases their experimental approach to blending music styles. Despite mixed initial reactions, they have garnered attention for their powerful vocals and intricate choreography.

THE GLOBAL IMPACT OF FOURTH-GENERATION K-POP

K-pop has entered a new phase of worldwide connection and influence with the rise of fourth-generation idols. This period has made K-pop a key part of the Korean cultural wave (known as **Hallyu 3.0**), working alongside Korean TV shows and movies to spread Korean culture globally. As a result, South Korea has become a must-visit destination for fans from around the world.

Fourth-generation K-pop stars have pushed the genre's influence beyond just music. They've become worldwide trendsetters in fashion and beauty, catching the attention of major luxury brands and creating new beauty standards across the globe. Their impact on style and beauty continues to drive the success of South Korean cosmetic products internationally, with their signature **"K-pop look"** becoming popular not just in Asia but increasingly in Western countries, too.

K-pop has grown into a powerful way to connect people with Korean language and culture. When fourth-generation idols perform and share their music, they inspire fans worldwide to learn Korean. This has led to steady growth in Korean language test applications, showing how K-pop helps connect different cultures through music.

The online world has opened up amazing possibilities. Through platforms like YouTube, Twitter, and TikTok, fourth-generation idols can reach fans directly across the globe, giving them an audience larger than any concert venue could hold. New technology also lets them try creative new ways to express themselves, making this a time of quick change and pushing boundaries in K-pop.

These fourth-generation stars are naturally skilled at using social media to connect with fans globally since they grew up with technology. However, they face significant challenges - there's pressure to debut new groups constantly and achieve immediate worldwide success. Creating endless content and staying connected with fans can make it hard to separate their work and personal lives, which can affect their well-being.

WHILE THE FOURTH generation's story is still being written, they've already built something that will have lasting effects. This era has brought rapid innovation, cultural exchange, and new horizons for K-pop worldwide. As the genre continues to grow, this generation has firmly established K-pop as more than just music - it's now a force that will shape global culture for years to come.

CHAPTER 10

THE GLOBAL SPREAD OF K-POP
THE HISTORY AND STRATEGIES BY REGION

K-POP'S EVOLUTION from a South Korean sensation to a worldwide cultural phenomenon shows its universal appeal — backed by savvy expansion strategies. It succeeded by understanding different audiences and adapting effectively to each market. This chapter explores K-pop's international journey, looking at key regions, their distinct cultural characteristics, and how K-pop successfully penetrated these diverse markets.

JAPAN: THE MARKET NEXT DOOR

Japan holds a special place in the global spread of K-pop for two main reasons: 1. It's South Korea's closest capitalist neighbor, and 2. It's one of Asia's leading cultural centers. For many years, K-pop companies used Japan as a testing ground to see if their artists could succeed beyond South Korea. The experience of promoting K-pop in Japan shaped how Korean artists would later approach fans in other countries.

Key Milestones and Cultural Impact

In the 1990s, Korean artists like **Seo Taiji and Boys** and **H.O.T**. made their first attempts to enter Japan, but found limited success. The turning point came with **BoA**'s debut in 2001. Her fluent Japanese and her album *Listen to My Heart* (2002) resonated with Japanese audiences, making her a household name and setting the stage for other Korean artists.

The 2000s saw Korean entertainment gain real momentum in Japan. Popular Korean TV shows, especially *Winter Sonata* (2002), ignited Japanese interest in Korean culture overall among the generation unencumbered by historical grievances and prejudices against Korea. This growing fascination helped boost both K-pop concert attendance and music sales. **TVXQ** (known as *Tohoshinki* in Japan) emerged as one of Japan's most successful foreign acts, leading to their historic Tokyo Dome concert in 2009.

The 2010s marked K-pop's breakthrough into Japan's mainstream music scene. Second-generation groups like **Girls' Generation** and **KARA** dominated the charts, with KARA's "Mister" dance becoming a cultural phenomenon. **BigBang**'s stadium tours drew massive audiences, cementing their place as one of Japan's favorite foreign acts. Even facing competition from popular Japanese groups like AKB48, K-pop maintained its appeal through superior performances and synchronized choreography.

In the late 2010s, **BTS** elevated K-pop's presence in Japan to unprecedented levels. Their albums *Face Yourself* (2018) and *Map of the Soul: 7 - The Journey* (2020) topped the *Oricon* **charts**. The rise of streaming platforms helped spread K-pop even further, as shown by BTS's "Lights/Boy With Luv" reaching No. 1 on the *Oricon Singles Chart*.

Cross-cultural collaboration has become the key to success, as demonstrated by **TWICE**, whose three Japanese members help them connect with local audiences through bilingual hits like "One More Time" (2017) and "Breakthrough" (2019). By 2024, **Stray Kids** emerged as a leading force in Japan's K-pop scene, drawing over 160,000 fans to their *SKZ Toy World* meet-and-greet. Major events like the **Music Bank Global Festival** and **Asia Star Entertainer Awards (ASEA)** held in Japan continue to showcase popular groups like **TXT,** Stray Kids, and **NewJeans**, proving the country's lasting enthusiasm for K-pop.

Notable Trends and Local Adaptations

K-pop groups make special efforts to reach Japanese audiences. They release Japanese-language songs and albums and spend time building relationships with local fans through special meet-and-greets and exclusive Japanese fan clubs. The polished, synchronized choreography and production style of K-pop continue to set it apart from Japanese pop idols, creating a strong niche in Japan.

K-pop's success in Japan is best evidenced by its inclusion in *Kōhaku Uta-Gassen (Red v. White Singing Contest)*, Japan's most important New Year's Eve music show. This program traditionally features Japan's biggest music stars of all generations, so having seven K-pop groups represented among its 44 performers in 2023 shows just how much Japanese audiences have embraced K-pop. It's no longer just a foreign fad — today, K-pop is undeniably mainstream in Japan.

Then there's **"Japanese K-pop"**: Japan-based K-pop groups like **NiziU** and **JO1**, made up of Japanese performers, formed by Korean entertainment companies like JYP Entertainment and CJ ENM (in partnership with *Produce 101 Japan*), and trained under the "K-pop system." These groups use K-pop's thorough training methods and performance standards, but focus on the Japanese market. This **"localized K-pop" model** combines K-pop's polished style with Japanese cultural elements, helping Korean companies grow their reach while giving Japanese audiences their own version of K-pop.

Challenges and Strategies

Occasionally, **political or historical tensions** between South Korea and Japan have created obstacles for K-pop. But entertainment companies have dealt with these situations smartly, by focusing on connecting directly with Japanese fans through bilingual releases, special fan clubs, and appearances on Japanese TV and media.

Key Events and Milestones — Summary

- **2002** — BoA's *Listen to My Heart* — First Korean album to top *Oricon*
- **2005** — TVXQ debuted their Japanese single *Stay with Me Tonight*
- **2009** — TVXQ's Tokyo Dome concert — First Korean group to perform at this iconic venue
- **2011** — Girls' Generation's Japanese debut album topped the *Oricon* charts and went double platinum
- **Late 2010s-Present** — BTS achieved unprecedented success with their Japanese albums *Face Yourself* and *Map of the Soul: 7 - The Journey*.
- **2020** — JO1 and NiziU, two of the first Japanese K-pop groups, debuted
- **2024** — Stray Kids' Kyocera Dome events with over 160,000 attendees

CHINA, HONG KONG, AND TAIWAN: ON THE OTHER SIDE OF THE WALL

China, Hong Kong, and Taiwan have been important but complicated markets for K-pop's international growth. While China's strict entertainment rules have made it difficult for Korean artists to perform there, K-pop groups still reach Chinese fans through social media and online platforms. Meanwhile, Hong Kong and Taiwan have become key markets where K-pop thrives openly, helping groups build strong relationships with Chinese-speaking fans and providing ways to reach wider Chinese audiences.

Key Milestones and Cultural Impact

The Korean cultural wave first reached Chinese-speaking regions through popular TV shows like *Winter Sonata*. This sparked interest in K-pop, particularly in Taiwan and Hong Kong. Early stars like **BoA** and **TVXQ** found success there, with TVXQ appearing on Taiwan's music charts and BoA releasing songs in Chinese to connect with local fans.

A major shift came when **Super Junior** created **Super Junior-M**, a subunit that performed in Mandarin. Their hit song "Super Girl" showed how successful K-pop could be across China, Taiwan, and Hong Kong. Taiwan became especially important, hosting many K-pop concerts and using its music charts to measure Korean artists' success.

EXO took K-pop's popularity even further by creating two versions of their group: one for Korea and one for Mandarin-speaking fans (**EXO-M**). Their songs "Overdose" and "Growl" became huge hits on Chinese music platforms like **YinYueTai**. EXO's member **Lay** became particularly successful in China, releasing popular Chinese albums like *Lose Control* (2016) and *NAMANANA* (2018) that helped connect K-pop with Chinese pop culture.

In the late 2010s, political issues between South Korea and China led to an unofficial "**Korean Ban**" after South Korea installed the THAAD missile system. This severely limited K-pop concerts, television appearances, and streaming content in China. However, fans found ways to stay connected through Chinese social media and music platforms like **Weibo**, **QQ Music**, and **Douyin**. Groups like **NCT** (which includes Chinese members) and **BLACKPINK** have maintained their popularity through their strong social media presence, even with these restrictions.

Notable Trends and Local Adaptations

K-pop companies use several smart approaches to reach fans in Chinese-speaking regions. They create songs in Mandarin, include Chinese performers in their groups, and stay active on Chinese social media. For example, **EXO's** Chinese member **Lay** helped the group connect with local fans, while newer groups like **aespa** and **Stray Kids** share special content on Chinese social media platforms. This helps them keep fans excited and engaged, even when faced with restrictions on live performances.

Challenges and Strategies

From soaring highs to sudden roadblocks, K-pop's journey in China reads like a dramatic K-drama plot twist. When the 2016 THAAD controversy slammed the door on traditional promotions, K-pop didn't miss a beat – it simply went digital. Rather than waving to fans from stadium stages, idol groups found themselves waving through screens, mastering the art of connecting with millions through Weibo posts and QQ Music livestreams, pivoting to digital fan meet-ups and concerts, and keeping fans connected despite regulatory limitations.

While mainland China presented its challenges, K-pop found its groove in the bustling streets of Hong Kong and the neon-lit cities of Taiwan. Hong Kong's vibrant music scene continues to welcome K-pop stars with open arms – you might catch **BIGBANG** setting the stage on fire one week and **GOT7** turning up the heat the next. Meanwhile, Taiwan has become K-pop's reliable dance partner, with passionate fans creating electric atmospheres at **BTS** and **TWICE** concerts that rival Seoul's energy. It's a testament to K-pop's superpower: the ability to adapt, evolve, and keep the music playing – no matter what political storms may brew.

Key Events and Milestones — Summary

- **2008** — Super Junior-M debuts with their Mandarin-language album *Me*, followed by the 2009 release of "Super Girl."
- **2012** — EXO debuts with a dual-unit concept, splitting into EXO-K for Korea and EXO-M for Mandarin-speaking markets. EXO-M's songs like "Growl" and "Overdose" quickly become hits in China.
- **2015–2018** — Lay, a Chinese member of EXO, launches a successful solo career in China, releasing Mandarin-language

albums like *Lose Control* (2016) and *NAMANANA* (2018), which top local charts.

- **2016** — The "Korean Ban" unofficially restricts K-pop concerts, television appearances, and streaming content in China, impacting K-pop's traditional promotional avenues.
- **2018–2019** — BLACKPINK becomes a leading K-pop act in China, achieving high streaming records on QQ Music and Weibo, despite restricted access to Korean content.
- **2020s** — Newer K-pop groups, including aespa and Stray Kids, maintain strong fan engagement in China through online fan meetings and concerts hosted on platforms like Weibo, Douyin, and QQ Music, adapting to the digital-only presence required by continued regulatory restrictions.

THE REST OF ASIA: SOUTHEAST ASIA AND BEYOND

Southeast Asia is like K-pop's home away from home. From the streets of Jakarta to the malls of Manila, Korean pop music has captured hearts across Indonesia, Malaysia, Singapore, Thailand, Vietnam, and the Philippines. These countries have become some of K-pop's biggest cheer-leaders outside Korea.

Key Milestones and Cultural Impact

It began in the early 2000s when Korean TV dramas first hit local screens. As viewers fell in love with Korean shows, they naturally got curious about Korean music, too. Early K-pop groups like **Super Junior**, **TVXQ**, and **BigBang** found their first international fans here, especially in Thailand, Malaysia, and the Philippines.

Throughout the 2010s, K-pop concerts in Southeast Asia became more common, with groups like **EXO**, **BTS**, and **TWICE** regularly performing in cities like Jakarta, Bangkok, and Manila. But it wasn't just about live shows – fans could now follow their favorite stars 24/7 through YouTube and Spotify, creating an even stronger connection to K-pop culture.

In 2023, K-pop's impact in Southeast Asia was highlighted by significant events like the **Asia Artist Awards** held in the Philippines, featuring top acts such as **Stray Kids**, **ITZY**, and **NewJeans**. Regional tours by groups like Stray Kids and ITZY also saw record-breaking attendance across major cities, proving that people still craved live performances in the post-pandemic world.

Notable Trends and Local Adaptations

When K-pop stars step onto Southeast Asian stages, they bring more than just music – they bring a genuine desire to connect. From mastering local greetings to weaving regional references into their shows, these thoughtful touches transform stadium-sized venues into intimate spaces where fans feel truly seen and appreciated. It's particularly magical when artists like BLACKPINK's **Lisa** switch between Korean and Thai, or when groups customize their performances for Indonesian or Filipino audiences, creating moments that celebrate local culture.

Today, K-pop is a thriving cultural phenomenon in Southeast Asia, with dedicated fan activities like **birthday cafes** and other fan-organized events illustrating the high level of engagement in the region. As K-pop evolves, Southeast Asia continues to be an indispensable market, blending online engagement with a strong demand for live performances.

India: The New Frontier

While K-pop first won hearts in Thailand and Indonesia, India is quickly becoming its newest success story. Thanks to social media, groups like **BTS** and **BLACKPINK** have attracted millions of Indian followers who stream their music videos and organize fan meetups. Though India hasn't hosted many live concerts yet (with **NCT 127**'s virtual performance at *All About Music* 2020 being a notable exception), the passionate fanbase shows just how much potential this market holds for K-pop's future.

Challenges and Strategies

K-pop companies are adapting their strategies to tackle key challenges across Asia: when venues are limited for live shows, they pivot to virtual concerts and online meet-ups; where language barriers exist, artists learn local greetings and content gets subtitled; in markets with restricted physical access, they focus on digital engagement through social media and streaming platforms; and in emerging markets like India, they partner with local brands and artists while building strong online communities.

Key Events and Milestones — Summary

- **Early 2000s** — K-dramas like *Winter Sonata* spark widespread interest in Korean culture across Southeast Asia.

- **2008** — Super Junior becomes one of the first K-pop groups to gain a major following in Southeast Asia.
- **2010s** — Regular K-pop tours by EXO, BTS, and TWICE establish strong fanbases in Southeast Asia.
- **2020** — NCT 127's virtual concert in India marks one of the first formal K-pop engagements with Indian fans.
- **2023** — Asia Artist Awards held in the Philippines feature Stray Kids, ITZY, and NewJeans.
- **2023** — Record-breaking Stray Kids concerts in Manila, Jakarta, and Bangkok reinforce the region's status as a vital market for K-pop.

THE UNITED STATES AND CANADA: BREAKING INTO THE WESTERN MARKET

K-pop's attempts to win over North American audiences have been an uphill battle. When Korean artists first tried breaking into the U.S. and Canadian markets, they faced tough challenges - from language barriers to different music industry practices. But patience and persistence paid off big time in the end: now K-pop stars headline major festivals, sell out arenas, and appear regularly on mainstream television shows like Jimmy Fallon and Good Morning America. What was once considered niche Asian pop music has established itself as a major force in North American mainstream entertainment.

Key Milestones and Cultural Impact

K-pop's journey into North America began with pioneers like the **Wonder Girls**, who in 2009 opened for the Jonas Brothers on their U.S. tour and charted on the *Billboard Hot 100* with "Nobody." In the same year, **BoA** attempted to replicate her Asian success with an English-language album, though these early efforts saw limited commercial impact. However, these experiences laid a foundation for future K-pop acts, who adapted their strategies to better connect with Western audiences.

In 2012, K-pop achieved a massive breakthrough with **PSY**'s viral hit "Gangnam Style," which became the first YouTube video to reach one billion views and peaked at #2 on the *Billboard Hot 100*. This viral sensation introduced K-pop to a truly global audience and kicked the doors wide open for the genre, particularly in Western markets.

The 2010s saw K-pop's breakthrough into the mainstream, led by groups like **BTS**. Their historic 2017 performance at the **American Music Awards** and appearances on major U.S. talk shows marked a turning point in K-pop's acceptance into American pop culture. BTS's continued success, including chart-topping hits like "Dynamite," cemented K-pop's place in the U.S. and Canada. **BLACKPINK** followed suit, making waves with their high-energy performance at Coachella in 2019, marking the first appearance by a K-pop girl group at this iconic festival.

In 2023, the Billboard Music Awards — one of the three most prestigious music awards in America alongside the Grammys and American Music Awards — established four new **K-pop-specific award categories**: Top Global K-pop Artist, Top K-pop Album, Top Global K-pop Song, and Top K-pop Touring Artist. This monumental move by Billboard wasn't made lightly—it signals K-pop's arrival as a solidly mainstream genre in America, following the path blazed by rap and Latin music in previous decades.

Coachella and Lollapalooza: Defining Moments in North America

K-pop's popularity in North America was further cemented by appearances at influential music festivals like Coachella and Lollapalooza, which attract global audiences and feature top-tier talent from across a wide variety of genres.

- **Coachella**, held annually in California's Indio Valley, is one of the largest and most prestigious music festivals in the U.S., drawing over 250,000 attendees. **BLACKPINK**'s groundbreaking performance in 2019 at Coachella introduced K-pop to a diverse crowd of music enthusiasts, earning rave reviews and substantial media coverage that helped broaden their fanbase. In 2023, **NewJeans** joined the lineup, further establishing the genre's place at the festival and connecting K-pop with a broader, trend-savvy audience.
- **Lollapalooza**, an annual four-day festival held in Chicago, draws hundreds of thousands of fans and is renowned for featuring influential acts across rock, hip-hop, electronic, and alternative genres. **TXT** made history as the first K-pop group to headline Lollapalooza in 2023, while **NewJeans** also made a well-received U.S. festival debut. In 2024, **Stray Kids** headlined the festival, underscoring K-pop's growing demand in the mainstream festival circuit.

These appearances at Lollapalooza and Coachella have allowed K-pop acts to reach beyond traditional fanbases, introducing the genre to attendees who might not otherwise engage with K-pop.

Notable Trends and Local Adaptations

To resonate with North American audiences, K-pop groups have produced English-language singles and made major media appearances. Platforms like YouTube, Spotify, and TikTok have further enabled K-pop's accessibility, while collaborations with Western artists—such as **BTS**'s "My Universe" with Coldplay—have bridged cultural divides and broadened K-pop's appeal.

Today, K-pop is an established force in North America, with sold-out stadium tours, dedicated fan communities, and regular coverage in mainstream media. The demand for K-pop at major festivals and concert venues reaffirms its lasting impact on Western music culture.

Challenges and Strategies

K-pop faced tough obstacles in North America - from language barriers to radio stations that were slow to embrace non-English music and a well-established, competitive music industry. Entertainment companies tackled these challenges head-on, getting their artists English coaching and teaming up with Western artists and producers.

While early groups tried going all-in with English albums, today's K-pop acts have found their sweet spot: staying true to their style while mixing in some English tracks. They've also mastered social media, using YouTube and TikTok to connect directly with fans instead of relying on traditional promotional channels, bypassing traditional gatekeepers. The rise of streaming services also helped, letting K-pop reach listeners without depending on radio play or conventional promotion channels.

Key Events and Milestones — Summary

- **2009** — Wonder Girls open for the Jonas Brothers.
- **2012** — Girls' Generation performs "The Boys" on *The Late Show with David Letterman.*
- **2012** — PSY's "Gangnam Style" video goes viral, achieving one billion views on YouTube; the song reaches #2 on the *Billboard Hot 100.*
- **2014** — KCON LA grows into a central festival for K-pop fans in North America.

- **2017** — BTS performs "DNA" at the American Music Awards, marking K-pop's major breakthrough into American pop culture.
- **2018** — BTS's album *Love Yourself: Tear* debuts at No. 1 on the Billboard 200, making them the first K-pop group to do so.
- **2019** — BLACKPINK performs at Coachella.
- **2019** — BTS becomes the first K-pop group to perform on *Saturday Night Live*, showcasing "Boy With Luv."
- **2020** — BTS's single "Dynamite" debuts at No. 1 on the *Billboard Hot 100*, marking another first for K-pop.
- **2021** — BLACKPINK's *The Album* debuts at No. 2 on the *Billboard 200*, the highest-charting album by a female K-pop group at that time.
- **2023** — TXT headlines Lollapalooza, with NewJeans also performing, representing the new wave of K-pop at U.S. festivals.
- **2023** — Billboard Music Awards establishes four K-pop-specific award categories.
- **2024** — Stray Kids headlines Lollapalooza; they also celebrate the boy band tradition at the American Music Awards 50th Anniversary Show by performing a blend of *NSYNC's "Bye Bye Bye" and their own "Chk Chk Boom."

UNITED KINGDOM, EUROPE, AND AUSTRALIA: K-POP'S EXPANDING GLOBAL REACH

The United Kingdom, Europe, and Australia have each played a unique role in K-pop's international journey, with each region offering opportunities and challenges for the genre's expansion. These regions demonstrate how K-pop has transcended linguistic and cultural barriers, solidifying its presence across Western markets with both large-scale concerts and dedicated local fanbases.

The United Kingdom: A Gateway to Europe

The U.K. has been a pivotal entry point for K-pop's European reach, thanks to its established music industry infrastructure and active media landscape. K-pop's presence in the U.K. began in the early 2000s, with fans discovering groups like **SHINee** and **Girls' Generation** through online communities and fan forums. K-pop's popularity grew with **BTS** and **BLACKPINK**'s highly publicized events, such as BTS's two sold-out nights at Wembley Stadium in 2019, a monumental achievement that elevated K-pop from a niche interest to a mainstream phenomenon in the British music scene. Events like **HallyuPopFest London** and the appearance of K-pop acts on BBC Radio 1 showed how far K-pop's reach had expanded across diverse demographics. In 2023, BLACKPINK became the first K-pop group to headline **Hyde Park's British Summer Time Festival**, with **Stray Kids** following in 2024, showing just how mainstream K-pop has become for British audiences.

Continental Europe: Expanding Horizons

K-pop has spread throughout Europe, adapting to each country's unique music scene. Streaming platforms like Spotify and YouTube have allowed K-pop to flourish in countries like France, Germany, Spain, and the Netherlands, where streaming numbers have surged over recent years. Major European cities now regularly host K-pop concerts, with Paris, Berlin, and Milan becoming popular tour stops. Special events like **KCON** in Paris and **Music Bank** in Berlin combine K-pop performances with Korean cultural experiences. Recently, **SEVENTEEN** made history by headlining **Lollapalooza Berlin** in 2024, showing how K-pop has become a major player in Europe's festival circuit.

Australia: Where East Has Met West Already

Australia has a unique place in K-pop's expansion as a Western market in the Asia-Pacific region. K-pop's initial fanbase in Australia developed through early exposure to K-dramas and channels like **SBS PopAsia**, which aired Korean music content regularly. The genre's visibility soared with **PSY**'s "Gangnam Style" in 2012, and by 2017, Australia hosted its first **KCON** in Sydney. Today, cities like Sydney and Melbourne host large K-pop concerts and dedicated stores selling K-pop merchandise. Australian fans have embraced K-pop culture, forming dance cover groups and organizing themed fan meetups, thanks to Australia's diverse population and its position between Asian and Western markets.

Notable Trends and Local Adaptations

K-pop groups connect with fans in the UK, Europe, and Australia through translated songs, TV appearances, and team-ups with local artists. Streaming services like Spotify and YouTube help K-pop reach fans everywhere, from small European towns to remote parts of Australia. Big festivals have also helped spread K-pop's popularity - groups like **Stray Kids** and **SEVENTEEN** performing at festivals like **Lollapalooza** in Paris and Berlin lets them reach new audiences. In

Australia, K-pop groups regularly sell out major venues in Sydney and Melbourne, showing their strong appeal down under.

Challenges and Strategies

K-pop faces unique challenges in the UK, Europe, and Australia that differ from those in the U.S., Japan, or China. In Europe, the variety of languages and cultures makes it harder to promote music across the region, and strong local music traditions can overshadow foreign genres. Australia's distance from major markets and preference for Western or local acts limits opportunities for exposure. Unlike Japan or China, where cultural and geographic ties help K-pop thrive, these regions lack the same natural connections. Additionally, Europe's indie and alternative music scenes, along with stereotypes about K-pop being overly manufactured, make it harder to win over mainstream audiences. To succeed, K-pop needs to focus on strategies like creating festivals and media channels for local fans, collaborating with Western artists, and tailoring promotions to fit each region's unique culture.

Key Events and Milestones — Summary

U.K. Milestones

- **2009** — K-pop's presence in the U.K. grows through fan forums and social media, with SHINee and Girls' Generation gaining popularity.
- **2012** — "Gangnam Style" reaches mainstream audiences.
- **2018** — BTS performs at London's O2 Arena, marking increased demand for large-scale K-pop events in the U.K.
- **2019** — BTS performs at Wembley Stadium, the first K-pop act to do so, drawing 120,000 fans over two nights.
- **2022** — HallyuPopFest London brings together multiple K-pop acts, further popularizing the genre.
- **2023** — BLACKPINK headlines BST Hyde Park in London; SEVENTEEN performs at Glastonbury, marking major milestones in U.K. festivals.
- **2024** — Stray Kids headlines BST Hyde Park.

Europe Milestones

- **2011** — K-pop expands in Europe through online platforms, reaching new audiences in France, Germany, and beyond.

- **2012** — Music Bank World Tour holds a concert in Paris, marking an initial entry into the European market.
- **2014** — SM Town Live tour draws thousands of fans to Paris.
- **2018** — Music Bank comes to Berlin, featuring acts including EXO, Wanna One, (G)I-DLE, Stray Kids, Jeon Somi, and Taemin.
- **2023** — Stray Kids headlines Lollapalooza Paris; Music Bank returns to Paris.
- **2024** — SEVENTEEN headlines Lollapalooza Berlin; KCON is held in Frankfurt; Music Bank comes to Antwerp, then Madrid.

Australia Milestones

- **2000s** — Early exposure through *SBS PopAsia* and local fan events creates an informed fanbase.
- **2012** — "Gangnam Style" becomes a cultural phenomenon, just like everywhere else.
- **2017** — KCON Australia debuts in Sydney, drawing large crowds.
- **2019** — BLACKPINK's *In Your Area* tour sells out in Sydney and Melbourne.
- **2022** — HallyuPopFest is held in Sydney.

LATIN AMERICA: A FLOURISHING HUB OF PASSIONATE K-POP FANDOM

Latin America has become one of K-pop's biggest markets outside Asia, with some of the most dedicated fans in the world. The region's love for dance and performance-driven music makes it a natural fit for K-pop's high-energy shows and complex choreography. This synergy has helped K-pop not only grow but thrive across the region, transforming it into a crucial part of the global K-pop landscape.

Key Milestones and Cultural Impact

K-pop first caught on in Latin America in the early 2010s when fans discovered groups like **Super Junior**, **BigBang**, and **Girls' Generation** on social media. Soon, cities like São Paulo, Mexico City, and Buenos Aires became must-stop locations for K-pop tours, with shows consistently selling out huge venues. The arrival of **KCON** festivals in Mexico (2017) and Chile (2018) showed just how important Latin America had become for K-pop.

Latin America's love for dance and performance arts was a natural fit with K-pop's emphasis on choreography, allowing the genre to connect instantly with audiences despite language differences. Local fans have developed a distinctive fan culture, organizing **flash mobs**, fan meetings, and social initiatives, while K-pop companies have responded by releasing Spanish versions of songs and creating content specifically for Latin American media.

The region has become a streaming powerhouse, with Mexico and Brazil among the top markets worldwide for K-pop on YouTube and Spotify. Newer groups like **Stray Kids** and **NewJeans** are hugely popular, and major K-pop companies like **HYBE** and **JYP** even opened offices in Mexico in 2024 to better connect with local audiences and support artist activities. Big events like **Music Bank** concerts in Chile and Mexico, **KCON Mexico**, and festival appearances keep bringing K-pop stars to Latin American fans, confirming the region as one of K-pop's most important markets.

Notable Trends and Local Adaptations

K-pop in Latin America has developed unique characteristics that reflect the region's cultural dynamics. Fan clubs organize large-scale events like K-pop **dance contests** and cultural festivals, often incorporating local dance styles with K-pop choreography. Spanish-language K-pop covers have become extremely popular on social media, with many Latin American artists gaining followers for their interpretations.

K-pop companies have adapted their strategies specifically for Latin America, releasing Spanish versions of songs (like **TWICE**'s "More & More" and **Stray Kids**' "Maniac") and collaborating with Latin artists. The region's strong social media presence has led to targeted digital marketing campaigns and exclusive content for Latin American platforms.

K-pop has also influenced local pop culture, with Latin American TV shows featuring K-pop segments and local entertainment companies developing training programs inspired by the K-pop system. An increasing number of artists of Latin American origin are debuting in K-pop groups.

Challenges and Strategies

K-pop's journey in Latin America hasn't always been smooth sailing. The sheer size of the region makes tours tricky and expensive to organize, while varying economic conditions mean not every fan can afford tickets or merch. But K-pop companies have gotten creative with solutions, rolling out multi-city tours and flexible pricing to reach more fans. They've also jumped into the digital world, hosting **virtual meet-and-greets** and creating online content that keeps fans connected even when they can't make it to live shows.

Working with local partners has been a game-changer in making K-pop more accessible. Companies team up with regional distributors to make merchandise more affordable and work with venues to keep ticket prices down. While the language barrier was once a big hurdle, companies now pour resources into Spanish content and local social media teams that really understand the culture. The fact that industry giants like HYBE and JYP have set up shop in Mexico shows just how serious they are about Latin America – it's not just another dot on the map anymore, but a key piece of their global puzzle.

Key Events and Milestones — Summary

- **2012** — Music Bank holds a concert in Chile, featuring Super Junior, marking the first large-scale K-pop event in the region.
- **2014** — Music Bank expands to Mexico City and Rio de Janeiro, Brazil.
- **2017** — KCON debuts in Mexico City, marking the first time the convention expands to Latin America, with groups like MONSTA X and ASTRO.
- **2018** — Music Bank returns to Santiago, Chile, with an expanded lineup.
- **2019** — BTS's *Love Yourself: Speak Yourself* tour stops in São Paulo, drawing massive crowds.
- **2022** — Music Bank returns to Santiago, with performances from (G)I-DLE and THE BOYZ.
- **2023** — The Rose performs at Lollapalooza Chile and Argentina, becoming the first Korean act to do so; Music Bank returns to Mexico City with ENHYPEN and STAYC.
- **2024** — RIIZE debuts at Tecate Emblema festival in Mexico City; HYBE and JYP open offices in Mexico City.

Fun Fact: Multiple studies have shown that the K-pop fandom has a white majority: white, non-Hispanic people make up anywhere from 43% to 46% of the global K-pop fandom as of 2023. Contrary to common belief, the numbers are much smaller in comparison for East Asian (7% to 17%), Southeast Asian (8.5% to 16%), Hispanic/Latino (9% to 16.5%), and multiracial (6%) fans.

K-POP'S GLOBAL STRATEGY: BEYOND KOREAN BORDERS

As K-pop continues its worldwide expansion, three key strategies have emerged as crucial elements in its international success: **diversification of talent**, **strategic collaborations**, and **regional adaptation**. These approaches have helped K-pop transcend its origins as a distinctly Korean product to become a truly global cultural phenomenon.

International Diversity in K-pop

The inclusion of non-Korean members in K-pop groups has evolved from a novelty to a strategic "must," expanding each group's reach to international fans through familiar faces. To recruit globally, K-pop companies have increased auditions outside of Korea, actively scouting talent in countries across Asia, the Americas, and Europe. This effort not only brings new languages and cultural perspectives into K-pop but also deepens the connection with international fans who see their own countries and cultures represented in the global phenomenon. Notable examples include:

- **BLACKPINK's Lisa:** Hailing from Thailand, Lisa has become an influential K-pop soloist, breaking records and serving as a global ambassador for brands like Celine and BVLGARI. Her dance videos attract millions of views, showcasing her role as a major cultural bridge.
- **Stray Kids' Australian Members (Bang Chan and Felix):** Their inclusion has been pivotal in appealing to English-speaking fans. Bang Chan's weekly "Chan's Room" live streams in English strengthened international fan connections and made the group more accessible to global audiences.
- **TWICE's Japanese Members (Momo, Sana, and Mina):** These members have been instrumental in TWICE's success in Japan, where the group consistently ranks high in Japanese music charts with their dedicated Japanese releases.
- **NewJeans' Hanni:** As a Vietnamese-Australian member, Hanni brings both Southeast Asian and Western perspectives to the group, contributing to their rapid global rise.

- **(G)I-DLE's Minnie (Thailand) and Yuqi (China):** These members expand the group's reach by appearing on variety shows in their home countries and speaking directly to local fans in their languages.

Strategic Global Collaborations

K-pop artists increasingly engage in high-profile collaborations with global musicians, creating projects that appeal to diverse audiences. Some notable collaborations include:

- **BTS and Coldplay's "My Universe" (2021):** This true collaboration with shared creative input reached No. 1 on the *Billboard Hot 100* and appealed to fans of both bands.
- **BLACKPINK's Collaborations (2020):** Working with artists like Selena Gomez on "Ice Cream" and Lady Gaga on "Sour Candy," BLACKPINK has helped make K-pop more visible to mainstream Western audiences.
- **LE SSERAFIM and Nile Rodgers' "UNFORGIVEN" (2023):** This collaboration with the legendary producer brought a fusion of K-pop and funk.
- **TXT and the Jonas Brothers' "Do It Like That" (2023):** TXT and the Jonas Brothers blended their musical styles to appeal to fans across multiple pop genres.

Regional Market Adaptation

To resonate with audiences in diverse regions, K-pop groups tailor their music, language, and promotion strategies to local cultures:

- **Language-Specific Releases:** TWICE's "The Feels," their first all-English single, was crafted for Western audiences while staying true to their style. Similarly, BTS released separate Japanese and English versions of "Butter" and "Permission to Dance" to maximize appeal across language markets.
- **Content Tailored to Local Fans:** K-pop groups make the extra effort to learn basic greetings and phrases in local languages for concerts, connecting with fans during international tours. For example, Stray Kids engages with Spanish-speaking fans through localized social media content.

- **The Sub-Unit System:** NCT's sub-units, such as NCT 127, NCT DREAM, and WayV, target Korean, Japanese, and Chinese audiences, respectively, through region-specific music, shows, and fan content.
- **Collaborations with Western Pop Culture:** SuperM worked with Marvel on promotional materials featuring Marvel-inspired visuals, blending K-pop with familiar Western pop culture elements to attract international fans.
- **Localized Digital Content:** BLACKPINK's music videos and NewJeans' promotions increasingly include multilingual captions and region-specific content, like TikTok challenges.
- **"Localized K-pop" — Localization through Local Member Groups:** An innovative approach within K-pop's regional strategy has been forming groups made up entirely of local members in non-Korean countries. NiziU and JO1, both formed in Japan through collaborations between Japanese and Korean entertainment companies, exemplify this strategy. With all local members trained under the K-pop model, these groups cater to local audiences with a relatable cultural perspective, blending familiar K-pop elements with native language and cultural nuances. Adaptations of the *Produce* TV series in countries like China (e.g., *Produce Camp*) and Vietnam (*Produce 101 Vietnam*) have similarly aimed to create locally tailored groups, demonstrating how K-pop continues to expand its global presence by integrating directly into regional entertainment ecosystems.

K-POP'S SECRET to success goes beyond catchy tunes and slick performances - the real magic is in adapting and connecting with fans worldwide. By mixing things up with diverse talent, trying new collaborations, and tweaking strategies for different markets, K-pop has managed to go global while keeping what makes it special. And with fresh faces like NewJeans and TXT trying out new ways to reach fans, K-pop's worldwide influence looks set to grow even stronger, shaped by what audiences want and where music is heading next.

CHAPTER 11

THE FUTURE OF K-POP
THE FIFTH GENERATION AND THE NEW WAVE: 2023-????

BY LATE 2022, K-pop was ready for its next big leap. The fourth generation had turned K-pop into a global sensation, but new tech and changing social attitudes pointed to more changes ahead. As 2023 kicked off, fresh idol groups started popping up, sparking talk among fans and industry experts about what they're calling K-pop's "fifth generation."

THE DAWN OF ANOTHER NEW ERA

The fifth generation of K-pop is stepping into a world where digital tech and global connection have hit new heights. With nearly 5 billion people on social media by 2023, and **AI**, **blockchain**, and **VR** going mainstream, the entertainment industry landscape has shifted dramatically. Music streaming has exploded too, with over 620 million paid subscribers changing how we experience music.

In this super-connected world, fifth-generation K-pop groups are emerging not just as musical acts, but as multi-dimensional digital entities. They are groomed to exist seamlessly across multiple platforms and media formats, blending real and virtual worlds in ways their predecessors couldn't even imagine.

DIGITAL IMMERSION FROM BIRTH

Born in the mid-2000s, these new idols grew up in a world that was already deeply connected. While calling them "**metaverse natives**" might be stretching it, they've been immersed in social media, streaming platforms, and online communities from a young age. It shows in how naturally they handle tech and connect with fans online.

K-pop training is evolving, too, but in subtle ways. While the basics - performance, language, and character - are still key, new skills are joining the mix. Trainees now learn the ins and outs of social media, pick up content creation skills for everything from vlogs to behind-the-scenes clips, and get schooled in global cultures. They're even dipping their toes into VR for fan meetings, though that's just getting started.

DEBUTING INTO A BORDERLESS WORLD

The fifth generation is launching into a K-pop scene that's truly global. Their seniors have paved the way for them, turning K-pop from a niche interest into something fans worldwide can't get enough of.

This borderless reality shows up everywhere in how new groups debut. Instead of just appearing in a TV show in Korea, they're increasingly likely to launch with simultaneous global events, leveraging advanced streaming technologies and virtual reality platforms to create shared experiences for fans worldwide. The groups themselves are more diverse, too, with members from all over bringing their own flavors to the mix.

Even what counts as a "debut" has changed. It's not just about dropping a single anymore - new groups are making a splash across platforms, from music to VR experiences, **webtoons**, and **NFTs**.

While it's hard to say exactly where one generation ends and another begins, it's clear K-pop is entering an exciting new chapter.

NOTABLE FIFTH-GENERATION GROUPS

While it's still early to definitively categorize groups as fifth generation, here are some notable recent debuts that might be considered part of this new wave:

ZEROBASEONE (2023-Present, WakeOne): Formed through the survival show *Boys Planet*, quickly gaining popularity with their fresh concepts and strong performances.

BoyNextDoor (2023-Present, KOZ Ent.): Known for their relatable, "boy-next-door" image combined with strong hip-hop influences.

Xikers (2023-Present, KQ Ent.): Boy group known for their intense performances and theatrical concepts, following in the footsteps of their senior group ATEEZ.

Kiss of Life (2023-Present, S2 Ent.): Girl group gaining attention for their retro-inspired sound and visuals, blending nostalgia with modern K-pop elements.

BABYMONSTER (2023-Present, YG Ent.): YG's new girl group, debuting with a blend of the company's signature sound and a fresh, youthful energy.

Fun Fact: BABYMONSTER, YG Entertainment's first girl group in seven years, held pre-debut evaluations live on YouTube, allowing fans to watch the selection process—a unique level of transparency for a K-pop group debut.

VCHA (2023-Present, JYP Ent.): The first K-pop girl group formed through a U.S. TV show, focusing strongly on the American market while maintaining K-pop production values. Their debut single, "Girls of the Year," charted on *Billboard's Hot 100*.

Plave (2023-Present, Vlast): Virtual boy group pushing the boundaries of AI and VR in K-pop, with fully computer-generated members and performances.

Meovv (2023-Present, Studio Mouse): A virtual girl group created using advanced AI technology, Meovv pushes the boundaries of digital performance in K-pop. With fully virtual members, their debut single "Digital Wonderland" captivated fans for its cutting-edge visuals and interactive fan experiences, showcasing a glimpse into the future of idol culture.

Zodiac (2023-Present, One Cool Jacso): Boy group with a unique astrological concept where each member represents a zodiac sign, showcasing individual personalities.

HORI7ON (2023-Present, MLD Ent.): A multinational boy group formed through *Dream Maker*, HORI7ON highlights the growing collaboration between Southeast Asia and K-pop. Their debut track, "Dash" showcases vibrant choreography and an energetic sound, appealing to both Korean and international fans.

EVNNE (2023-Present, Jellyfish Ent.): Formed from *Boys Planet* contestants, EVNNE debuted with "Trouble," combining emotional storytelling and polished performances. Their focus on sincerity and artistry positions them as a standout boy group in the fifth generation.

FANTASY BOYS (2023-Present, PocketDol Studio): Debuting with "New Tomorrow," FANTASY BOYS impressed with their strong vocals and intricate choreography. Their performances demonstrate the promise of a group poised to make an impact in the fifth generation.

ADYA (2023-Present, Starting House Ent.): Known for their youthful and colorful image, ADYA debuted with a bright and cheerful concept. Their track "Periwinkle" captures a playful charm, making them a refreshing addition to the fifth generation of K-pop.

KATSEYE (2024-Present, JYP Ent.): Blends traditional Korean cultural elements with futuristic themes. Their debut single, "TTBKK," garnered attention for its unique fusion of *pansori*-inspired vocals with modern pop production.

TWS (2024-Present, Pledis Ent.): Boy group that gained attention for their self-produced music and involvement in all aspects of their debut album creation.

ILLIT (2024-Present, Belift Lab): The girl group debuted with an AI-integrated concept, focusing on global appeal from the start. Their debut showcase featured innovative use of hologram technology, setting a new standard for high-tech K-pop performances.

Riize (2024-Present, SM Ent.): Boy group known for their "cyberpunk idol" concept. Their debut showcase featured an interactive virtual reality experience for fans.

NEXZ (2024-Present, JYP Ent.): Boy group showcasing JYP's new direction in male idol concepts. Known for their synchronized choreography and storytelling through music videos.

WHERE K-POP IS HEADED

As K-pop continues to evolve, the industry faces both exciting opportunities and significant challenges. The potential fifth generation of K-pop idols is entering a world vastly different from their predecessors, shaped by rapid technological advancements and shifting global dynamics.

Technological Integration and Innovation

The future of K-pop is likely to be characterized by deeper integration of cutting-edge technologies:

- **Virtual and Augmented Reality:** VR and AR could transform how we experience concerts. SM's *Beyond LIVE* shows are already showing us what's possible, featuring real-time interactions between idols and fans alongside spectacular visual effects.
- **AI and Machine Learning**: These technologies might personalize fan experiences, help create music, and even bring virtual idols to perform alongside human artists.
- **Blockchain and NFTs**: Blockchain technology might transform fan engagement, offering unique digital collectibles and allowing fans to have a stake in their favorite groups' activities.
- **Metaverse Concerts:** As virtual shared spaces become more sophisticated, we may see K-pop concerts held entirely within digital worlds, making shows accessible to fans everywhere.

Evolution of Sound and Performance

K-pop's sound will likely keep evolving, blending traditional Korean elements with global influences. We'll probably see more cross-genre and international collaborations, pushing the boundaries of what we consider K-pop.

Live shows will incorporate more tech elements too, with holograms and AR becoming regular features.

Co-ed Groups: A New Frontier?

Mixed-gender groups in K-pop have remained relatively rare. While groups like **Kard**, **Triple H**, and **AKMU** have found success, they haven't reached the heights of leading boy or girl groups. Several factors play into this:

- **Marketing challenges:** Companies find it easier to market to specific demographics with single-gender groups.
- **Fanbase dynamics:** Traditional K-pop fan culture has mainly centered around same-gender idol admiration or opposite-gender attraction.

- **Choreography limitations:** It's challenging to create choreography that works for both male and female idols equally well while keeping things appropriate.
- **Cultural factors:** Some markets still hold conservative attitudes about mixed groups.

However, changing dynamics might open new doors for co-ed groups. As global audiences gain influence, old barriers may matter less. Mixed-gender groups offer unique dynamics and can explore new concepts that single-gender groups cannot. They also have the potential to break down gender stereotypes within K-pop.

While it's uncertain whether co-ed groups will become a major trend in K-pop's future, the industry's constant drive for innovation suggests that we may see more experiments in this direction. As K-pop continues to push boundaries and redefine itself, co-ed groups might find new avenues for success as the industry evolves and transforms.

Changing Landscape of Fan Engagement

The way idols and fans connect is set to evolve in interesting ways:

- **Enhanced Interactivity:** Social media and fan communication apps may become more sophisticated, potentially using AI to break down language barriers for real-time translations.
- **Fan Participation:** Blockchain-based voting systems could allow fans to influence creative decisions, from concept choices to promotions.
- **User-Generated Content:** Fan-created content might become more integrated into official promotions, blurring the lines between fans and creators

Challenges and Ethical Considerations

The industry faces some real hurdles going forward:

- **Market Saturation:** With the industry more crowded than ever, standing out becomes increasingly challenging for new groups.
- **Mental Health:** As the pace of the industry accelerates, protecting idols' mental well-being remains crucial.
- **Sustainability:** Balancing the demand for physical albums and

merchandise with environmental concerns presents new challenges.

- **Data Privacy:** The use of AI and data analytics in fan engagement raises important questions about privacy and data security.
- **Global Tensions:** As K-pop's influence grows worldwide, navigating international politics becomes trickier

Industry Reforms

K-pop might see some significant changes in how things work:

- **Training System:** AI-assisted programs could help identify and nurture talent more efficiently. Virtual training academies might open up opportunities for aspiring idols worldwide.
- **Contractual Relationships:** There may be a shift towards more transparent and idol-friendly practices, with companies prioritizing the long-term well-being of their artists.
- **Global Diversity:** The industry could become even more diverse, with more international trainees bringing fresh perspectives to K-pop.

THE FUTURE of K-pop holds endless possibilities, driven by technological innovation, cultural evolution, and global expansion. As the industry navigates challenges and seizes new opportunities, it stands poised to redefine not just Korean music, but the global entertainment industry as a whole.

OUTRO

As our journey through K-pop's history comes to a close, one thing becomes clear: we're not just witnessing the success of a music genre – we're watching the evolution of global popular culture itself.

From its humble beginnings in the aftermath of the Korean War to its current status as a worldwide cultural force, K-pop has consistently defied expectations and broken down barriers. Those who dismiss K-pop as a "passing fad" fundamentally misunderstand its deep-rooted impact on the very fabric of entertainment.

The mere fact that Billboard Music Awards decided to establish four new K-pop-specific award categories in 2023 speaks volumes about K-pop's permanent place in the music industry, joining established genres like rap and Latin music in America's musical mainstream.

The secret to K-pop's success lies not just in its catchy melodies or synchronized dance moves, but in its ability to adapt and innovate while maintaining its unique identity. It's a perfect blend of Korean traditional values and global popular culture, of artistic expression and technological advancement, and of entertainment and social connection.

Looking ahead, K-pop stands at the threshold of yet another transformation. As artificial intelligence, virtual reality, and blockchain technology reshape the entertainment world, K-pop is once again positioning itself at the forefront of innovation. The fifth generation of K-pop artists is already experimenting with new ways to connect with fans and push creative boundaries, suggesting that the industry's most exciting chapters may still lie ahead.

But perhaps most importantly, K-pop has shown us that music can transcend language, culture, and geography to create meaningful connections between people around the world. In an era often marked by division, K-pop reminds us that shared passion and creativity can bring people together in powerful ways.

Whether you're a long-time fan or new to the world of K-pop, this story demonstrates something remarkable: when artistic vision meets dedication, when tradition embraces innovation, and when fans and artists come together with a shared passion, something truly magical can happen. K-pop isn't just changing the music industry – it's showing us what's possible when we dare to dream beyond borders and boundaries.

The beat goes on, the dance continues, and somewhere in the world, another person is about to discover the irresistible charm of K-pop for the very first time. As we look to the future, it's clear that K-pop's journey is far from over. It will face challenges and undergo transformations, but one thing is certain: it's here to stay.

Welcome to the future of global entertainment – it speaks Korean, but its language is universal.

APPENDIX

IDOLS & GROUPS BY

		SM Entertainment	YG Entertainment	JYP Entertainment	DSP Media	Cube Entertainment
1st Gen. (1997-2002)	Boy	H.O.T., Shinhwa, Fly to the Sky	1TYM	Rain (solo), g.o.d.	Sechs Kies	
	Girl	S.E.S., Hyoyeon (solo), BoA (solo)			Fin.K.L.	
2nd Gen. (2003-2011)	Boy	TVXQ, Super Juinior, Lay (solo), SHINee	BIGBANG, Taeyang (solo), Se7en (solo), G-Dragon (solo)	2PM	SS501	BEAST/Highlight
	Girl	Girls' Generation, f(x)	2NE1	Wonder Girls, Miss A	KARA, Rainbow, Lee Hyori (solo)	4Minute, HyunA (solo)
3rd Gen. (2012-2017)	Boy	EXO, NCT	WINNER, AKMU, iKON	GOT7, DAY6		BTOB, PENTAGON
	Girl	Red Velvet, Taeyeon (solo)	BLACKPINK, CL (solo)	Sunmi (solo), TWICE		
4th Gen. (2018~2022)	Boy		TREASURE	Stray Kids, Xdinary Heroes		
	Girl	aespa		ITZY, NMIXX		(G)I-DLE, LIGHTSUM
5th Gen. (2023-)	Boy	Riize		NEXZ		
	Girl		BABYMONSTER	KATSEYE, VCHA		

GENERATION AND AGENCY

FNC Entertainment	Starship Entertainment	HYBE Labels	Others
			PSY (Yedang & Cream, signed with YG in 2010), Drunken Tiger (Jungle), Nell (Woolim Ent.)
			Baby V.O.X (DR Music)
F.T. Island, CNBLUE			U-KISS (NH Media), MBLAQ (J. Tune Camp), INFINITE (Woolim Ent.), ZE:A (Star Empire Ent.), TEEN TOP (Top Media)
	SISTAR	After School (Pledis Ent.)	IU (solo, LOEN Ent.), T-ara (MBK Ent.), Brown Eyed Girls (Nega/APOP), SECRET (TS Ent.), Apink (IST Ent.)
SF9	MONSTA X	BTS (Big Hit Ent.), SEVENTEEN (Pledis Ent.)	ASTRO (Fantagio), Wanna One (YMG Ent.), The Boyz (IST Ent.), Jackson Wang (solo, Team Wang), VIXX (Jellyfish Ent.)
AOA		GFRIEND (Source Music), fromis_9 (Pledis Ent.)	MAMAMOO (RBW Ent.), Dreamcatcher (Dreamcatcher Company)
P1Harmony	Cravity	TXT (Big Hit Ent.), ENHYPEN (Belift Lab)	ATEEZ (KQ Ent.), WOODZ (solo, Yuehua Ent.), ONEUS (RBW Ent.), DKZ (Dongyo Ent.), Kang Daniel (solo, Konnect Ent.), KINGDOM (GF Ent.)
	IVE	LE SSERAFIM (Source Music), NewJeans (ADOR)	LOONA (Blockberry Creative), Hwasa (solo, RBW/P Nation), EVERGLOW (Yuehua Ent.), SOMI (solo, The Black Label), STAYC (High Up Ent.), PURPLE KISS (RBW Ent.), TRI.BE (TR Ent.), Kep1er (WakeOne Ent.)
		TWS (Pledis Ent.), BoyNextDoor (KOZ Ent.)	ZEROBASEONE (WakeOne Ent.), Xikers (KQ Ent.), Plave (Vlast), Zodiac (One Cool Jacso), HORI7ON (MLD Ent.), EVNNE (Jellyfish Ent.), FANTASY BOYS (PocketDol Studio)
		ILLIT (Belift Lab)	Kiss of Life (S2 Ent.), Meovv (Studio Mouse), ADYA (Starting House Ent.)

K-POP FANDOM NAMES

Group	Fandom Name	Group	Fandom Name	Group	Fandom Name
1TYM	Hip Hop Village	(G)I-DLE	Neverland	PSY (solo)	PSYcho
2NE1	BLACK JACK	Girls' Generation	SONE	PURPLE KISS	PLORY
2PM	HOTTEST	g.o.d	fan god	Rainbow	Rainnous
4Minute	4NIA	GOT7	iGOT7	Red Velvet	ReVeluv
aespa	MY	H.O.T.	Club H.O.T.	Riize	BRIIZE
After School	Play Girlz	Hwasa (solo)	TWITS	S.E.S	Friend
AOA	AOE	HyunA (solo)	A-ing	Se7en (solo)	Lucky 7
ATEEZ	ATINY	iKON	iKONic	Sechs Kies	Yellow Kies
Baby V.O.X	Baby Angels	ILLIT	GLLIT	SEVENTEEN	CARAT
BABYMONSTER	MONSTIEZ	INFINITE	Inspirit	SF9	FANTASY
BEAST/Highlight	B2UTY/Light	ITZY	MIDZY	SHINee	SHAWOL
BIGBANG	VIP	IU (solo)	Uaena	SISTAR	Star1
BLACKPINK	BLINK	IVE	DIVE	SS501	Triple S
BoA (solo)	Jumping BoA	KARA	Kamilia	STAYC	SWITH
BoyNextDoor	ONEDOOR	KATSEYE	EYEKONS	Stray Kids	STAY
BTOB	Melody	Kep1er	Kep1ian	Super Juinior	E.L.F
BTS	ARMY	KINGDOM	KINGMAKER	T-ara	QUEEN'S
CL (solo)	GZB	Kiss of Life	KISSY	THE BOYZ	The B
CNBLUE	Boice	LE SSERAFIM	FEARNOT	TREASURE	Treasure Maker
Cravity	LUVITY	LIGHTSUM	SUMIT	TVXQ	Cassiopeia
DAY6	My Day	LOONA	Orbit	TWICE	ONCE
Drunken Tiger	MFBTY	MAMAMOO	MooMoo	TWS	42
ENHYPEN	ENGENE	Miss A	Say A	TXT	MOA
EVERGLOW	FOREVER	MONSTA X	MONBEBE	VCHA	VLIGHTS
EXO	EXO-L	NCT	NCTzen	Wanna One	Wannable
f(x)	ME U	New Jeans	Bunnies	Weeekly	Daileee
Fin.K.L	FINKY	NEXZ	Nex2y	WINNER	INNER CIRCLE
Fly to the Sky	Fly High	NMIXX	NSWER	Wonder Girls	Wonderful
fromis_9	flover	ONEUS	TO MOON	Xikers	roady
G-Dragon (solo)	Applers	P1Harmony	P1ece	ZEROBASEONE	ZEROSE
GFRIEND	BUDDY	Plave	PLLI	Zodiac	X-BLISS

GLOSSARY

AEGYO: Cutesy and charming behavior, often exhibited as fan service through facial expressions, gestures, and a higher-pitched voice.

All-kill: A song that reaches #1 on all major Korean music charts simultaneously.

"Behind": Short for "behind-the-scenes," referring to off-camera moments from events, rehearsals, or photo shoots. These moments are often shared through vlogs, documentaries, or social media to give fans a look at idols' candid sides.

"Bias": Your favorite member in a K-pop group.

"Bias Wrecker": A member of a K-pop group who unexpectedly catches your attention and makes you question your loyalty to your original bias.

Bubble: A subscription-based messaging app launched by Dear U, allowing K-pop fans to receive personalized messages, photos, and updates from their favorite idols. Fans can reply, creating the feeling of a private conversation, though responses are not directly viewed by idols.

"Comeback": A K-pop term for an artist or group's release of new music, often accompanied by promotions, performances, and concept teasers. Unlike the general English usage, it doesn't imply the artist was inactive or absent for a long time—it's used for every new release, even if it's just months after the previous one.

"Dance Practice": Videos where idols perform their full choreography in a studio setting, usually wearing casual workout or athleisure outfits. Unlike music videos or TV performances, which often include non-dance scenes or focus on individual members, dance practice videos showcase the entire group's synchronized movements.

Ending Fairy: The member who gets the final close-up shot in a stage performance, often striking a dramatic or memorable pose for the camera. Ending Fairy moments are highly anticipated by fans.

Fan Meeting: A special event where idols and fans interact in a more personal setting, often including Q&A sessions, games, mini-performances, and fan engagement activities. Fan meetings can range in scale from small, intimate gatherings to large events that resemble concerts, complete with elaborate stages and performances.

Fan Sign Event: An intimate event where fans meet idols individually to have albums or merchandise signed. Fans often exchange short, meaningful conversations with idols, making it a cherished experience for dedicated supporters.

Fancam: Video recording of a performance, usually at a concert or live event, that focuses on a single member of a group.

Fanservice: Gestures or actions by idols meant to entertain or please fans, such as physical contact or playful interactions between group members, heart signs, or humorous skits.

Finger Heart: A small hand gesture where the thumb and index finger cross to form a tiny heart shape, symbolizing love or affection. Popularized by K-pop idols and Korean celebrities, it began in South Korea around the early 2010s and has become a globally recognized sign of appreciation and connection within K-pop culture.

"Girl Crush": A K-pop concept that highlights bold, confident, and empowering female personas, appealing to both male and female fans. It features strong choreography, edgy styling, and themes of independence and self-assurance, often contrasting with cute or innocent concepts.

"Hard Carry": A term used when an idol "carries" the team, i.e., makes an exceptional contribution to a group's success, such as through standout vocals, visuals, or leadership during a critical moment or performance.

Hi-Touch Event: A fan interaction event where attendees briefly meet idols and exchange a quick high-five or light touch. These events are typically held after concerts or fan meetings, offering fans a personal and memorable experience with their favorite idols in a controlled setting.

Hiatus: A temporary break from group or individual activities, often due to health issues, personal reasons, group restructuring, or even scandals and controversies. Hiatuses may last weeks, months, or even years.

Hubae (후배): Korean for "junior," referring to someone with less experience or who started later in a shared field, such as school, work, or the entertainment industry. In K-pop, idols who debuted earlier are considered *sunbaes* (seniors) to those who debut later, and respecting *sunbaes* is an important part of industry etiquette.

Hyung (형): Korean for "older brother," used by males to address an older male sibling or friend. Male idols often use this term for older group members or older friends in the industry.

KCON: An annual convention celebrating Korean pop culture and entertainment, featuring concerts, fan meetups, panels, and cultural showcases. Launched in 2012 in California by CJ ENM, it aimed to connect global fans with K-pop and Korean culture. Today, KCON has expanded to multiple countries, becoming a premier global event for K-pop and Hallyu enthusiasts.

Lead Vocalist/Rapper/Dancer: Among the best singers/rappers/dancers of the group, but rank below the main singer/rapper/dancer.

Leader: The member responsible for guiding and representing the group.

Light Stick: A special light-up wand used by fans during concerts to show their support for their group. Each group has its own unique design.

Main Vocalist/Rapper/Dancer: The most skilled and prominent singer/rapper/dancer in the group.

"Maknae" (properly pronounced *'mang-nae'* in Korean): The youngest member in the group.

"Member Shine": Moments where a specific idol is highlighted in a performance, either through solo lines, screen time, or a special performance that showcases their unique skills or personality.

"Ment": Short for "comment," refers to the talking segments during K-pop events such as concerts where idols interact with the audience.

"Mission": A task or challenge —often silly— given to idols, commonly in survival shows, variety programs, or fan events.

Music Bank: A weekly South Korean music show produced by KBS, airing since 1998. It features live performances by popular K-pop artists and ranks songs based on a chart system combining digital sales, broadcast points, and viewer votes.

Music Bank World Tour: A worldwide live concert tour of Music Bank (see above). The tour stages live performances, featuring multiple K-pop acts, in various locations outside of South Korea. Since July 2011, the Music Bank World Tour has been held in multiple cities across Asia, Europe, and Latin America, with an estimated global live audience of 200,000.

Noona (누나): Korean for "older sister," used by males to address an older female sibling or friend. Male idols often use "noona" for older female fans or idols, adding a layer of warmth and respect in fan interactions.

Noona Fan (누나 팬): An older female fan who admires or supports younger male idols.

Oppa (오빠): Korean for "older brother," used by females to address an older male sibling, friend, or idol they admire. It is commonly used affectionately by fans when referring to male idols.

OT: Stands for "One True"; indicates support for the original lineup of a group. Ex: OT8 refers to all eight members of a group, emphasizing support for the entire lineup.

Point Choreography: The signature dance move of a song, often repeated in the chorus and highlighted in performances. Designed to be catchy and visually striking, point choreography frequently goes viral, with fans worldwide emulating the moves in covers and social media challenges, solidifying its place in K-pop culture.

Produce: A South Korean reality TV series that aired from 2016 to 2019, focusing on the formation of temporary K-pop groups. Trainees from various agencies competed in challenges, with winners chosen through public voting. The show produced successful groups like I.O.I, Wanna One, IZ*ONE, and X1, shaping the fourth generation of K-pop. Its success led to international spin-offs, including *Produce 101 China* and *Produce 101 Japan,* expanding its influence globally. The series ended after controversies over vote manipulation but remains a landmark in idol group formation.

Sasaeng: An obsessive fan who crosses personal boundaries to invade idols' privacy, often through stalking or other extreme behavior.

"The Seventh Year Itch": A term in K-pop referring to the challenges idol groups often face around their seventh year, typically due to the expiration of standard seven-year contracts. Many groups disband or undergo significant changes during this period as members reassess their careers. The term highlights the industry's competitive nature and the difficulty of maintaining long-term group success.

Selca (셀카): A shorthand for "self-camera," meaning a selfie. On Selca Day, fans post their own selfies alongside photos or mementos of their favorite idols, creating a fun and interactive tradition in K-pop fandoms.

Sming (스밍): Short for "streaming," referring to the act of fans continuously streaming an idol's songs or videos on platforms like YouTube and Spotify to boost chart performance and rankings.

Stan: A particularly dedicated and enthusiastic supporter of an artist or group; a combination of "stalker" and "fan."

Streaming Party: A collective fan effort to stream an idol's music or videos simultaneously to achieve milestones, such as higher chart positions or view counts. Often organized through social media campaigns.

Sunbae (선배): Korean for "senior," referring to someone with more experience in a shared field. In K-pop, *sunbaes* are idols who debuted earlier and often act as mentors or role models to newer idols (*hubaes*).

Ultimate Bias: A fan's favorite idol of all time across all groups, ranking above their regular biases.

Unnie (언니): Korean for "older sister," used by females to address an older female sibling or friend. Female idols also use "*unnie*" for older group members, reflecting closeness and hierarchy.

V Live: A live streaming app where K-pop idols interact with fans in real-time. (V Live has been fully integrated into the Weverse platform as of the end of 2022.)

"Visual": The most physically attractive member of the group.

REFERENCES

14 Korean dramas starring popular K-pop idols that you ... https://www.vogue.in/culture-and-living/content/korean-dramas-starring-popular-k-pop-idols-that-you-can-watch-on-netflix-and-viki

Asian superstars Wonder Girls open for Jonas Brothers https://www.seattletimes.com/entertainment/asian-superstars-wonder-girls-open-for-jonas-brothers/

The Brutal Daily Schedule Of A K-Pop Idol Trainee ... https://www.koreaboo.com/stories/lesserafim-sakura-idol-trainee-kpop-debut-documentary-world-oyster-brutal-daily-schedule/

The "BTS Effect" on South Korea's Economy, Industry and ... https://shadow-twts.medium.com/the-bts-effect-on-south-koreas-economy-industry-and-culture-975e8933da56

BTS Rules the Night at the American Music Awards https://variety.com/2021/music/news/bts-american-music-awards-1235117136/

Burning Sun Scandal: A Timeline of Allegations, Arrests & ... https://www.billboard.com/music/music-news/burning-sun-scandal-timeline-seungri-jung-joon-young-8503818/

Colonialism and Popular Music https://www.atlantis-press.com/article/125964851.pdf

Confucianism Influence on Korean Pop Culture - Academia.edu https://www.academia.edu/39218730/Confucianism_Influence_on_Korean_Pop_Culture#~:text=In%20sum%2C%20as%20seen%20in,pop%20music%20and%20the%20artists.

Crafted for the Male Gaze: Gender Discrimination in the K- ... https://vc.bridgew.edu/cgi/viewcontent.cgi?article=2492&context=jiws

Encyclopedia Britannica. "K-pop." Britannica. Accessed November 23, 2024. https://www.britannica.com/art/K-pop

The Fourth Generation of K-Pop: The Next Level https://hallyuism.com/2022/02/05/the-fourth-generation-of-k-pop-the-next-level/

From cultural phenomenon to state strategy: South Korea's ... https://www.aa.com.tr/en/asia-pacific/from-cultural-phenomenon-to-state-strategy-south-koreas-hallyu-policy/2973735

Gov't to campaign for K-pop industry to go green https://www.koreatimes.co.kr/www/nation/2024/09/113_376718.html

How Social Media Helped K-Pop Become a Global ... https://www.nyucommclub.com/content/2021/11/24/how-social-media-helps-k-pop-become-a-global-phenomenon

How VR is revolutionising K-pop experiences and bringing ... https://www.tatlerasia.com/lifestyle/entertainment/bts-blackpink-vr-concerts-online-fanmeets#~:text=As%20VR%20technology%20continues%20to,the%20setlist%20in%20real%20time.

The influence of Confucianism on Korean traditional music https://catalogue.nla.gov.au/catalog/1655924

INTRODUCTION — SM Entertainment https://www.smentertainment.com/en/company/introduction/

JYJ and S.M. Entertainment end three-year legal spat https://www.koreaherald.com/view.php?ud=20121130000586

Korea Traditional Musical Instruments https://artsandculture.google.com/story/korea-traditional-musical-instruments-national-gugak-center-gugakwon/QQXBWFVCGDVvKQ?hl=en

Korean ballad - Wikipedia https://en.wikipedia.org/wiki/Korean_ballad#~:text=Gaining%20popularity%20alongside%20trot%20in,popularized%20in%20main-stream%20Korean%20culture.

Korean Crisis and Recovery https://www.imf.org/external/pubs/nft/seminar/2002/korean/

K-pop is making billions for South Korea - Asia Fund Managers https://asiafundmanagers.com/us/kpop-and-economic-impact-on-south-korea/

Kpop Trainee's Daily Schedule - kpopatmosphere https://kpopatmosphere.wordpress.com/2020/07/11/kpop-trainees-daily-schedule/

Looking Back On Wonder Girls' 'Nobody,' A Decade Later https://www.billboard.com/music/music-news/wonder-girls-nobody-10-year-anniversary-k-pop-hot-100-chart-8476481/

Mental Health & the Lack of Mental Health Care in the K-Pop ... https://youreignhere.medium.com/mental-health-the-lack-of-mental-health-care-in-the-k-pop-industry-ac743ebf034a

Mirotic https://en.wikipedia.org/wiki/Mirotic

Prelude to War of K-Pop: H.O.T. vs Sechs Kies - UoH https://uofhorang.com/prelude-to-war-of-k-pop-h-o-t-vs-sechs-kies/

Psy's 'Gangnam Style' Invented YouTube's Billion Views Club https://www.billboard.com/music/pop/psy-gangnam-style-10th-anniversary-youtube-billion-views-club-1235115043/

Sasaeng fan - Wikipedia https://en.wikipedia.org/wiki/Sasaeng_fan#:~:text=A%20sasaeng%20or%20sasaeng%20fan,with%20sasaeng%20-fans%20is%20stalking.

Sechs Kies https://en.wikipedia.org/wiki/Sechs_Kies

Seo Taiji and Boys https://en.wikipedia.org/wiki/Seo_Taiji_and_Boys

Sorry, Sorry (Super Junior song) https://en.wikipedia.org/wiki/Sorry,_Sorry_(Super_Junior_song)

South Korea in 1992: A Turning Point in Democratization https://www.jstor.org/stable/2645284

TAG Launches New Asian Touring Sector https://www.tag-group.com/group/news/tag-launches-new-asian-touring-sector

Teddy Park production discography https://en.wikipedia.org/wiki/Teddy_Park_production_discography

'They use our culture': the Black creatives and fans holding ... https://www.theguardian.com/music/2020/jul/20/k-pop-black-fans-creatives-industry-accountable-race

This Is South Korea's K-pop Soft Power Moment https://thediplomat.com/2022/02/this-is-south-koreas-k-pop-soft-power-moment/

HOPE YOU ENJOYED THE SHOW!

If this book helped deepen your K-pop experience, would you take a moment to share your thoughts? Even a quick star rating or a few words can help other fans discover the magic of K-pop culture.

Just click/scan the QR codes below or click "Write a product review" on your Amazon order.

If you would like to purchase another copy, just click/scan:

감사합니다 (Thank you!) from The Hallyu Press Team 🤍

If you liked this one, you may want to check out our other books:

KOREAN FOR K-POP FANS: Master Basics of Hangul, Grammar, and Pronunciation — Understand Song Lyrics, Get Jokes, and Sing Along with Your Favorite Idols

COREANO PARA K-POP FANS: Domina lo básico del Hangul, la gramática y pronunciación - Entiende la letra de las canciones y los chistes, y canta con tus ídolos favoritos

ALSO...

EL FENÓMENO DEL K-POP: Sus orígenes, su evolución y futuro - Recorre la historia de los idols de primera a quinta generación y explora las fuerzas detrás de esta sensación global

AND

THE ULTIMATE K-POP DICTIONARY: From Hangul to Konglish – Decode Fandom Slang, Idol Culture, Song Lyrics, and Industry Jargon with These 500+ Words and Phrases Commonly Used in the World of K-pop